THE SOUTH WEST Way

1994

THE COMPLETE GUIDE TO THE SOUTH WEST COAST PATH, GREAT BRITAIN'S LONGEST TRAIL.

0850 - 506135.

Peninsula
Press

THE SOUTH WEST WAY ASSOCIATION

Registered as a charity (No. 266754)

The Association formed to promote the interests of users of the
South West Way (South West Coast Path)

CHAIRMAN

Philip CARTER, Beaver Cottage, 36A Old Exeter Road,
Newton Abbot, Devon TQ12 2NE.
Tel: (0626) 52905

TREASURER

Derek HEXTER, F.C.A.,
43 Torquay Road,
Newton Abbot,
Devon TQ1 2JB.
Tel: (0626) 52162

SECRETARY

Eric WALLIS
'Windlestraw',
Penquit,
Ermington,
Devon PL21 0LU,
Tel: (0752) 896237

MEMBERSHIP SECRETARY

Mrs Mary MACLEOD
1 Orchard Drive,
Kingskerswell,
Newton Abbot,
Devon TQ12 5DG.
Tel: (0803) 873061

Published jointly by:
The South West Way Association and Peninsula Press Ltd
P.O. Box 31, Newton Abbot, Devon TQ12 5XH.

Trade Sales and Distribution:
Barnicoats, Parkengue, Penryn, Cornwall

Printed in England by BPCC Wheaton, Exeter, Devon.

ISBN 1 872640 27 3

Originated by Greenshires Icon, 84 Longbrook Street, Exeter, Devon.

Jacket design by A&B Creative Services, Kingskerswell, Devon.

Jacket photograph of Yearnor Woods, near Porlock Weir
by Martin Collins

CONTENTS

INTRODUCTION

The South West Way is one of the official long distance trails funded by the Countryside Commission and maintained on its behalf by County Councils and National Park authorities. The route is waymarked by the distinctive acorn symbol.

The South West Way is by far the longest of the Official Long Distance trails; it runs from Minehead in Somerset right round the South-Western peninsula to South Haven Point on the south side of Poole Harbour in Dorset. We ourselves reckon this is 613 miles, others differ but all agree it is a fair step! A recent contour count indicates you will climb over 91,000 ft which is three times Mount Everest.

This Footpath Guide attempts to provide in one single unit all the basic information you need to walk the path. The information is updated annually and members (see Invitation to Membership, page 95) are advised by Newsletters of important changes during the year.

We try to provide the basic information, that is sometimes so difficult to assemble for other Long Distance trails, in just one small booklet.

The path was enacted in the National Parks and Access to the Countryside Act of 1949. It must seem amazing therefore, to those who do not know the fact, that it is still unfinished after forty years.

It is sometimes called the South-West Peninsula Coastal Path, which is more of a mouthful. Parts of it are disguised as the Somerset and North Devon, North Cornwall, South Cornwall, South Devon and Dorset Coastal Paths. None of this administrative nonsense was intended by the originators of the path and walkers may find such divisions a nuisance. More to the point, these, and even smaller administrative divisions have been allowed in the past to spawn very different standards of routing and maintenance. However, now that The Heritage Coast Service and footpath wardening is becoming more universal, standards are improving all around.

A survey established that one of the chief joys of those accomplishing the Pennine Way was the sense of achievement; of a challenge met. What of our path which is twice as long and requiring far more total effort? More seriously because of its length, few will be able to undertake to walk it as a whole. That is why as much as possible of this guide is written to be just as useful to those who only wish to walk parts of the path.

Which Way Round? Unless we undertook to write the whole guide both ways we had to make a decision to keep all the information in sequence starting from one end or the other. In fact, bearing in mind the shape of the South West peninsula, to go round approximately clockwise or anti-clockwise. For the day walker it does not really matter very much at all – considerations as to where you are, transport, etc. will largely dictate your decision. However, the hardy soul setting out to do the whole path may well prefer to have the prevailing wind from the South West more often behind. To do this it is necessary to walk from Minehead to Poole or in other words anti-clockwise. This point made us decide to make our path order therefore that way round and all information is listed that way – anti-clockwise, but now see below.

The path does undoubtedly pass through some of the finest coastal scenery in Europe and, with its enormous variety and contrast between bustling resort and quiet cove, is a never ceasing source of delight. Its other main feature is the tremendous amount of interest of all kinds along its way.

This path is the longest Long Distance Trail – we think it is the finest we hope you will too! We certainly know of no other Long Distance Trail that has as much contrast and variety as ours. Try it!

THE OTHER WAY ROUND

In this book the description of the South West Way is from Minehead–Land's End–Poole. The Association has now written a description of the Trail for those walking the other way. It deals only with the path so this annual guide will be necessary for all the other information. The 'other way round' supplement is available from the membership secretary or secretary at £2.30 including postage.

WEATHER

The South West Way is more exposed to wind than any other Long Distance Trail – Pay attention to gale forecasts as well as rain. Along some sections, strong winds can be dangerous especially when rounding exposed headlands and crossing bridges. A high backpack can act like a sail. Detailed forecasts are available on: (0898) 500 405 (Somerset) / (0898) 500 404 (Devon & Cornwall) / (0898) 500 403 (Dorset),

A WORD TO BEGINNERS

Long Distance Path Walking

Please, these words are not for those hardy veterans who have all the gear, have done several paths already, and know all about it. We will only say to them at least read the second paragraph of 'Grading' near the beginning of the 'Trail Description' section. However, we do get a number of letters each year from those who have not ventured before on Long Distance Paths and need some advice. This we are pleased to try and provide and we do hope those who read this will find it helpful. However, it is easy to miss out things that folk wish to know, so if you who are new read this, and are still baffled, please write to us and we will try to provide the answers. As well as perhaps helping you, it will enable us to improve this section for another year and so be of help to more people.

For Those Who Have Never Been Walking

Have you been walking at all before? If the answer is no, do not for heaven's sake try and plan several days' continuous walking. You need to do some day walks – there are some very good ones on the coast – first. Better still, look for the sections marked "Easy" – start at one end and stop and turn back before you have half had enough. We say before half because it is always better to do a bit less and really enjoy it.

You can soon progress to setting out to walk a whole section either by using two cars or using public transport. One point here – if possible use the public transport to go out and walk back to your car or base. This means that you do not get yourself in a position of having to race the clock if you should take a bit more time than you thought.

If you are walking on your own, do please take additional care for, as you will appreciate, if you fall or twist an ankle there can be problems. If you are on your own therefore, you should leave a note with someone to make sure that you arrive at your destination. Not everyone is happy walking on their own and can feel lonely. There is also an added problem that you may try to do too much, so please bear this in mind.

There is no need to buy expensive equipment for the easy sections at the start. A pair of stout shoes and a rainproof is all you need. As you progress, a small rucksack or haversack for 'eats' will be needed next.

Obviously if you can join a walking club and go out with them you will collect lots of friendly advice on all sorts of gear you may care to purchase as you become more serious about walking. Maps, guides, etc., are all listed in their appropriate sections.

For Those Who Have Walked, But Not On Long Distance Trails

Day walking on Long Distance Trails is really no different from any other kind of day walking. It is only when you contemplate several days' continuous walking that other considerations arise and there are some pitfalls which even quite experienced day walkers often overlook.

Do not be too ambitious in the mileage you plan. Do not carry too much weight of gear.

Having stated the two big points, we will elaborate. You will not be able to accomplish in daily mileage the same amount you normally cover in a day walk! You will have to settle for less! The first reason is that you will be carrying more equipment; you must for instance, have a complete change of clothing and footwear, possibly nightwear and toilet kit. For this you need a bigger rucksack so you will be carrying quite a bit more weight than you normally do. Secondly, there is what we call the 'wear' factor. For the first few days until you are really fit, it is just simply more tiring having to walk each day. The last point could be called the 'interest' factor. Usually, if you are walking a Long Distance Path, you are further from your home base in fresh fields and pastures new; there is more to see so you will need more time to look around.

If you usually accomplish 15 miles a day – aim, say, for 12. This is particularly important if you are booking ahead. You can find yourself tied to a treadmill which you cannot get off. Booking ahead has the advantage that you know there is a bed ahead. On the other hand, it does mean even if you are tired, have developed blisters, and the weather is diabolical, you have to go on! Be guided too by our 'Trail Description' section, the terrain you are tackling. 6 miles, say, of a 'Severe' section can equal in effort 10-12 miles of an 'Easy' one.

We have stated you must carry more gear and this is true. Having said that, think long and hard about every item you imagine you may need. You will be surprised – you may find you will not want it at all! Watch particularly those extras such as cameras and binoculars – they are often a source of considerable weight. One little additional point, many rucksacks, even modern ones, are not as waterproof as you think. A plastic liner which can be obtained quite cheaply from rambling shops, etc., as an additional inner layer may save you that most unpleasant discovery after a long day spent in the rain that your only change of clothing is no longer dry. We would also recommend that in addition to this liner your dry clothing should then be enclosed in further plastic bags to ensure dryness. Trainer shoes are useful for wearing at the end of the day and can be worn on some parts of the path.

A sensible idea before undertaking a full Long Distance Footpath holiday is to take, say, a long weekend of two or three days first, walking continuously as a practice.

We are sometimes asked if you require a map as well as a guide book and our advice is certainly yes. A good guide such as Bartholomew gives you a considerable amount of information but, strange as it may seem, it is at its most useless when you actually get lost! Agreed, one does not get as badly lost on the Coastal Path as you can on inland ones but nonetheless a map is an asset. Furthermore many walkers derive much interest from looking at their route in relation to the rest of the countryside on ordinary walks and the same applies just as much, if not more so, on a Long Distance Path. The National Trail Guides offer a partial solution with their maps; but even these are not as useful as a Map Sheet.

Another point to watch especially on our Coastal Path is the availability of refreshment. At main holiday times, you will get it nearly everywhere except for the few places we especially mention in our 'Trail Description' section. Out of season, you will find it in surprisingly few places on long stretches of coast. The usual remarks about carrying stand-by supplies, therefore, certainly apply; better to carry an extra couple of bars of chocolate than to go hungry.

BADGES

We offer specially designed badges for the South West Way.

Cloth badges for rucksack, anoraks, etc. £1.00 inclusive of postage and packing

We think these badges are attractive – we hope you will too. Available both for members and non-members alike.

CERTIFICATES

These are now available to persons who have walked the whole path. Free to members. £1.00 to non-members.

BOOKS, etc.

This list is not exhaustive, there are a number of other books available but we have tried hard to list all those which are really useful and even those not really useful that you might think would be!

PUBLICATIONS ARE AVAILABLE DIRECT FROM YOUR ASSOCIATION, FOR QUICK SERVICE PLEASE WRITE TO THE MEMBERSHIP SECRETARY, MRS M. MACLEOD, 1 ORCHARD DRIVE, KINGSKERSWELL, NEWTON ABBOT, DEVON TQ12 5DG.

South West Way – Minehead to Penzance

South West Way – Penzance to Poole.

Both these excellent pocket sized books are by Martin Collins. We can recommend them as most useful. Available from Cicerone Press, 2 Police Square, Milnthorpe, Cumbria, LA7 7PY at £8.95 each (Postage and packing 55p per book). Also available from the South West Way Association.

National Trail Guides – published by Aurum Press in association with the Countryside Commission and Ordnance Survey. Available from the Countryside Commission Publications, Printworks Lane, Levenshulme, Manchester M19 3JP; The Ordnance Survey, Romsey Road, Maybush, Southampton SO9 4DM; most bookshops and our own association from the Membership Secretary. These are good guide books with good maps. An excellent venture by the producers involved.
Minehead to Padstow by Roland Tarr
Padstow to Falmouth by John Macadam
Falmouth to Exmouth by Brian Le Messurier
Exmouth to Poole by Roland Tarr
Price £8.99 + 50p postage from our Membership Secretary.

500 Mile Walkies by Mark Wallington (from bookshops only). Published by Arrow.
An amusing account of a walk by the author, accompanied by a dog, along the whole of the path.

Walk the Cornish Coastal Path by John Mason. This is a Bartholomew Map and Guide at £4.99. An excellent guide to all of the Cornish Coast. From Membership Secretary (Post 50p).

South West Cornwall Guide including accommodation, available free from: The Tourism Officer, Council Offices, Camborne. Tel: (0209) 712941.

Twelve Walks in South West Cornwall. Price £1.80 plus postage from The Tourism Officer, Council Offices, Camborne. Tel: (0209) 712941.

LANDFALL WALKS BOOKS – Bob Acton of Devoran has written eleven splendid books that contain well over 100 circular walks in Cornwall. These feature sections of the coast path throughout the county. They will enable walkers to progress along the coast path by basing themselves at one location. Write to Landfall Publications, Landfall, Penpol, Devoran, Truro, TR3 6NW for full list, or telephone 0872 862581.

Footpath Touring with Ken Ward. Land's End and The Lizard. Price £3.75 including postage. Available direct from 'Sea Chimney', South Down, Beer, EX12 3AE. An excellent guide to this section of the path by one of the co-authors of the well-known Letts Guides.

Walk South Devon Coastal Path and Dartmoor by John Mason and Eric Hemery. This is a Bartholomew Map and Guide at £5.99. An excellent guide to the South Devon Coast. Available from Membership Secretary (Post 50p).

Two Moors Way (now illustrated) – by Devon Area Ramblers Association – Price £1.50. This is not our path. One is enough! But we do stock the Official Guide. This describes the path from Lynmouth in North Devon to Ivybridge near Plymouth – and very well done it is too. (Available from South West Way Association. Postage 40p. Write to Membership Secretary.)

The South Devon Coast Path. An Aerofilms Guide featuring spectacular aerial photo-maps and landscapes covering the walk from Lyme Regis to Plymouth. Price £8.99. Published by Ian Allen Ltd, Terminal House, Shepperton, Surrey, TW17 8AS (0932 228950).

SOUTH WEST WAY PUBLICATIONS

Path Descriptions by our association are very detailed accounts on all aspects of short sections of the coast path and include maps and illustrations. They cover in great detail what cannot be included in the guide book.

These Path Descriptions are all priced at 60p + 19p postage for up to 2 copies, 29p for up to 4 copies, 36p for up to six copies and 43p for up to 12 copies. All are available from the Membership Secretary, Mrs M. Macleod, 1 Orchard Drive, Kingskerswell, Devon, TQ12 5DG. Telephone: (0803) 873061.

FOOTPATH DESCRIPTIONS

NORTH DEVON AND SOMERSET

Minehead to Lynmouth

Lynmouth to Ilfracombe

Ilfracombe to Croyde Bay

Croyde Bay to Appledore

Appledore to Hartland Point

Hartland Point to Marsland Mouth

(List continued overleaf.)

CORNWALL

Marsland Mouth to Crackington Haven
Crackington Haven to Tintagel
Tintagel to Port Isaac
Port Isaac to Padstow
Padstow to Porthcothan
Porthcothan to Newquay
Newquay to Perranporth
Perranporth to Portreath
Portreath to Hayle
Hayle to Zennor
Zennor to Sennen Cove
Sennen Cove to Porthcurno
Porthcurno to Penzance
Penzance to Porthleven
Porthleven to The Lizard
The Lizard to Helford
Helford to Place House
Place House to Mevagissey
Mevagissey to Fowey
Fowey to Looe
Looe to Cremyll (River Tamar)

SOUTH DEVON

Plymouth (River Tamar) to Wembury
Warren Pt. Wembury to Bigbury
Bigbury to Salcombe
Salcombe to Torcross
Kingswear (River Dart) to Brixham
Brixham to Shaldon
Shaldon to Sidmouth
Sidmouth to Lyme Regis

DORSET

Weymouth to Lulworth Cove
Lulworth Cove to Kimmeridge
Kimmeridge to South Haven Point

HISTORICAL

The South West Way 125 Years Ago
The Queen v Ames (1840-3). A Legal
Marathon on the Devon/Dorset border

NATIONAL TRUST BOOKS

The National Trust Book of Long Walks by Adam Nicholson.
Published by Weidenfeld & Nicholson – price £12.95.
This includes The South West Way as well as a number of other Long Distance Footpaths, official and unofficial. It has a fairly brief description of the Path and it does have the most magnificient collection of photographs we have yet seen.

The National Trust Guide to the Coast by Tony Soper.
Published by Webb & Bower – price £14.95
This is really a general guide to the coast but, because a lot of National Trust coastal properties are in the South West, this area features largely in the text and in the superb photograph illustrations.

Coastline. The National Trust Coast of Devon. Published by Devon Books – price £3.95.

NATIONAL TRUST REGIONAL INFORMATION OFFICES:

Devon Information Office, Killerton House, Broadclyst, Exeter, Devon EX5 3LE (Tel: Exeter (0392) 881691).

Dorset & Somerset Region Information Office, Stourton, Warminster, Wilts. BA12 6QD (Tel: Bourton, Dorset (0747) 840560).

Cornwall Information Office, The Estate Office, Lanhydrock Park, Bodmin, Cornwall PL30 4DE (Tel: Bodmin (0208) 74281).

BRITISH RAIL

Throughout the year there is an excellent service of direct InterCity trains between London (Paddington) and Torbay, Plymouth and Cornwall. There are also regular InterCity Cross Country services linking Birmingham, the North West, the North East and Scotland with Torbay, Plymouth, Cornwall, Bournemouth and Poole. All these services have catering facilities available for the whole

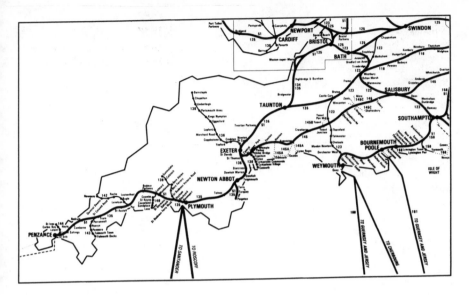

or part of the journey. During May to September, InterCity services are considerably augmented on Saturdays (check your local railway station) and seat reservations are essential on many of these trains to avoid overcrowding and ensure passengers a comfortable journey (Direct InterCity trains between London (Paddington) and Torbay run only in the summer timetable as do InterCity services to Newquay).

All daytime services between Paddington, Plymouth and Penzance are operated by InterCity 125 trains with the journey time to Torquay and Plymouth just over 3 hours from London.

There is also a regular Wessex Electric service from London (Waterloo) to Bournemouth, Poole and Weymouth for those who intend to walk the Dorset end of The South West Way. East Devon is served by a two-hourly Network Express service from Waterloo to Axminster (for Lyme Regis and Seaton) and Honiton (for Sidmouth).

Regional Railways have greatly improved their service in the South West and can now offer a direct new Class 158 link between Paignton and Cardiff. The new Class 158, air-conditioned 90mph trains also link Penzance with South Wales, Birmingham and Swindon. New rolling stock has been introduced on most branch lines in Devon and Cornwall and make reasonable connections into and out of the long distance InterCity services. Most of these branch lines are open on Sundays during the summer months and the first four also have a limited Sunday service during the winter months.

Westbury–Yeovil–Weymouth   Liskeard–Looe
Exeter–Barnstaple   Par–Newquay
Exeter–Exmouth   Truro–Falmouth
Newton Abbot–Torquay–Paignton   St Erth–St Ives
Plymouth–Gunnislake

A wide variety of attractive reduced-rate fares are often available in the popular holiday areas during the summer months as are a wide variety of Rover tickets. Details of these may be readily obtained on enquiry at stations and Travel Centres.

Private Branch Line Railway

Bishops Lydeard to Minehead – The West Somerset Railway PLC run steam trains through twenty scenic miles to Minehead. Bishops Lydeard is four miles outside Taunton and easily accessible by bus. The service operates between March and October. For details contact the company at 'The Station', Minehead TA24 5BG (Tel: 0643 704996).

Paignton to Kingswear (Dartmouth) – For the rambler who is also a railway enthusiast, the Paignton and Dartmouth Railway is a 'must'. This most attractive line runs from Paignton to Goodrington, Churston and Kingswear and operates preserved Great Western steam locomotives and rolling-stock.

The line passes through some delightful coastal and river scenery, and a trip on the railway could easily be combined with a walk to make a very pleasant day out. It operates from March to December. For details contact – Queens Park Station, Torbay Road, Paignton TQ4 6AF (Tel: 0803 555872).

Bodmin Parkway to Bodmin Town is a service that could prove useful for those requiring bus transport to the coast. Contact Tel: 0208 73666.

BUS SERVICES

LISTED BELOW, IN PATH ORDER, ARE THE MAIN OPERATORS RELEVANT TO THE SOUTH WEST WAY.

SOMERSET:
For services from Taunton to Minehead, Lyme Regis and Weymouth, Southern National Ltd, Bus Station, Tower Street, Taunton, TA1 2EU – Taunton 272033.

Somerset County Council also produce public transport timetables for the County in 8 areas, available from Tourist Information Centres, Libraries or from the Public Transport Section, County Hall, Taunton, TA1 4DY – Taunton 255696.

NORTH DEVON:
For services from Barnstaple to Lynton, Bideford and Westward Ho!, Red Bus North Devon Ltd, Coney Avenue, Barnstaple, EX32 8QJ – Barnstaple 45444.

Devon County Council also produce a timetable covering the North Devon area. For information on services in the area Devon County Council Devon Bus enquiry line – Exeter, Barnstaple or Plymouth 382800.

CORNWALL:
Cornwall County Council produce a comprehensive Public Transport Timebable annually, generally in time for the Summer period. As services may change during the currency of the timetable it is advisable to check with the operators concerned. Available from Public Transport Section, Cornwall County Council, County Hall, Truro, TR1 3BE.

There is no County bus enquiry number in Cornwall. Western National information is available from 21A Pydar Street, Truro, TR1 2AY – Truro 40404.

SOUTH HAMS:
For services from Plymouth to Wembury, Kingsbridge and Dartmouth, Western National Ltd, Laira Bridge, Plymouth, PL4 9LP – Plymouth 222666.

TORBAY:
For services around Torbay, including Brixham, Paignton and Torbay, Bayline Ltd, Regent Close, Shiphay, Torquay, TQ2 7AN – Torquay 613226

For services around Exeter including services to Exmouth and Sidmouth, Devon General Ltd, Bus Station, Paris Street, Exeter, EX1 2JP – Exeter 56231

For details of all services within Devon. Devon County Council, Devon Bus enquiry line – Exeter, Barnstaple or Plymouth 382800, 0830–1700 Monday–Friday.

DORSET:
For services from Lyme Regis to Bridport and Weymouth, Southern National Ltd, 80 The Esplanade, Weymouth, DT4 7AA – Weymouth 783645

For services from Swanage to Poole and Bournemouth via Sandbanks, Wilts and Dorset Ltd, Towngate House, 2–8 Parkstone Road, Poole, BH15 2PR – Poole 673555.

Dorset County Council produce a rural bus timetable available from, Public Transport Section, County Hall, Dorchester, DT1 1XJ – Dorchester 251000.

USEFUL ADDRESSES

Countryside Commission, South West Region, Bridge House, Sion Place, Bristol, BS8 4AS.

Country Wide Holidays Association, Birch Heys, Cromwell Range, Manchester, M14 6HU. Tel: 061 224 2887.

Exmoor National Park Authority, Exmoor House, Dulverton, Somerset TA22 9HI.

HF Holidays Ltd, Imperial House, Edgware Road, Colindale, London NW9 5AL.

Ramblers' Association, 1/5 Wandsworth Road, London SW8 2XX.

South East Cornwall Discovery Centre, Millpool, West Looe, PL13 2AF (0503 262777).

COUNTY COUNCILS

Somerset County Council, County Hall, Taunton, TA1 4DY.

Devon County Council, County Hall, Exeter, EX2 4QW.

Cornwall County Council, County Hall, Truro, TR1 3BE.

Dorset County Council, County Hall, Dorchester, DT1 1XJ.

Addresses of Ramblers' Association contacts in the West Country

All path obstructions or other problems not on the Coast Path itself should be addressed to the relevant County address.

Devon – Mrs E. M. Linfoot, 14 Bladen Cottages, Blackborough, Cullompton, EX15 2HJ.

Cornwall – Mr N. H. Taylor, The Shealing, Veryan Green, Truro, TR2 5QQ.

Dorset – Mr B. Panton, 5 Nicholas Gardens, Ensbury Park, Bournemouth, BH10 4BA.

Somerset – Mr S. Barnard, 11 Gordons Close, Taunton, TA1 3DA.

MAPS

Metric 1:50,000 Map

The Metric 1:50,000 Landranger Series needed to cover the coast from Minehead in Somerset to Studland in Dorset are as follows, working round the coast from Minehead.

181	Minehead & Brendon Hills	200	Newquay & Bodmin
180	Barnstaple & Ilfracombe	201	Plymouth & Launceston
190	Bude & Clovelly	202	Torbay & South Dartmoor
200	Newquay & Bodmin	192	Exeter & Sidmouth
204	Truro & Falmouth	193	Taunton & Lyme Regis
203	Land's End & The Lizard	194	Dorchester & Weymouth
204	Truro & Falmouth	195	Bournemouth & Purbeck

The two tourist 1" maps of Dartmoor and Exmoor available are of no advantage except that Exmoor could be used instead of Map 181 and nearly all 180.

Pathfinder 1:25,000 Map

The following is a list of 1:25,000 (2½" to the mile) scale of the Second Series (Pathfinder) sheets which are currently available.

1215/SS 84/94	Minehead	1366/SW 83	Falmouth & St Mawes
1214/SS 64/74	Lynton/Lynmouth	1361/SW 94/SX 04	Mevagissey & Tregony
1213/SS 44/54	Ilfracombe/Lundy	1354/SX 05/15	St Austell & Fowey
1233/SS 43/53	Barnstaple/Braunton	1355/SX 25/35	Looe
1254/SS 42/52	Bideford/Atherington	1356/SX 45/55	Plymouth
1253/SS 22/32	Clovelly	1362/SX 54/64	Newton Ferrers & Thurlestone

1273/SS 21/31	Kilkhampton	1367/SX 73	Salcombe
1292/SS 20/30	Bude/Holsworthy	1363/SX 74/84	Kingsbridge/Stoke Fleming
1310/SX 19	St Gennys	1358/SX 85/95	Dartmouth & Brixham
1325/SX 08/18	Camelford	1351/SX 86/96	Torbay
1337/SW 87/97	Padstow & Wadebridge	1342/SX 87/97	Newton Abbot & Teignmouth
1346/SW 86/96	Newquay	1330/SY 08/18	Sidmouth
1352/SW 75	Perranporth	1316/SY 29/39	Lyme Regis/Axminster
1359/SW 54/64	Camborne (North)	1317/SY 49/59	Bridport
1365/SW 63	Camborne (South)/Hayle	1331/SY 58	Abbotsbury
1364/SW 33/43	St Ives & Penzance (North)	1343/SY 67/77	Weymouth/Portland
1368/SW 32/42	Land's End/Newlyn	1332/SY 68/78	Weymouth (North)/
1369/SW 52/62	Helston & Prussia Cove		Dorchester (South)
1372/SW 61/71	Lizard Point	1333/SY 88/98	Wareham
1370/SW 72/82	Helford River	1334/SY 87/97	Studland/Brownsea Island

Outdoor Leisure Maps

There are two Ordnance Survey Outdoor Leisure Maps 1:25,000 available for parts of the path. These are South Devon (No. 20) and Purbeck (No. 15). A double sided map (No. 9) – Exmoor is due in the Spring.

As far as the South Devon one is concerned, we cannot really recommend it to anyone. There is so much of the South Devon Path which is missing and the fact that the Brixham peninsula is shown as an inset makes it difficult to use.

The Purbeck Map which covers the stretch from Durdle Door, West of Lulworth Cove to South Haven Point at the southern side of the mouth of Poole Harbour is more useful – the path at least being shown in one piece.

Where an area of a Pathfinder map is completely covered by an outdoor leisure map, then the Pathfinder map may not be available.

OFFA'S DYKE: MORE THAN A PATH!

For 1,200 years the term 'Offa's Dyke' has meant the great earthwork thrown up by the powerful ruler of Mercia (central England) to mark the boundary with the Welsh and as such it has also colloquially come to refer to the Anglo-Welsh boundary. In the last forty years a new meaning has come to the term with the designation of the Offa's Dyke Long Distance Footpath in 1949. It took 22 years from designation to the opening in 1971 and here lies the origin of another meaning to 'Offa's Dyke', the Association. This was originally set-up to act as a pressure group to push for the necessary works and the opening to take place. Since 1971 Offa's Dyke Path has become one of the best used of the National Trails, and a name known to most 'serious' walkers. The Association has had no mean success itself with, now, over 1,000 members.

But why have a long distance footpath along this particular route? The historic border it may be but it follows no obvious physical feature. Offa's Dyke Path as a walking route is something else, in one word, Variety. The Welsh Border is, for Britain, lonely country and some of the most attractive and unspoilt moorland, rolling hills and farmland are crossed by the Path between the tourist areas of the Wye Valley and the North Wales coast. Across the plains of Gwent, over the Black Mountains, the river valleys and hills of Radnor, the Severn and Dee valleys, the limestone hills round Llangollen and the Clwyddian ridges: the list of varied attractions is long. For nearly half the route the earthwork is your companion, often 20 feet from ditch to top even after twelve centuries of erosion. Many castles and abbeys lie near the route and though the 177 miles can be covered in a week, most visitors will sensibly prefer a more leisurely walk.

But why an Offa's Dyke Association? And, in particular, what was the need for this voluntary pressure group to continue beyond the official opening of the Path? We foresaw some of the needs of visitors to the Path that official facilities and services could not meet and we correctly anticipated a minor boom in walking and other tourism where there had been little before. Also inevitably there would be a different approach to the Path from walkers and from historians, from visitors and from those who lived and worked there. If we could cover this range of interests then harmony in development, rather than areas of conflict would be more likely.

Our Offa's Dyke Centre at Knighton, run with local authority aid, serves well over 20,000 people each year. Most want to know about accommodation and so we publish annual 'where to stay' and camping lists. Additionally we issue guides, 'strip maps' of the route, point to point route notes in both directions, circular walks and alternative routes based on the Path, also town trails and history notes. We sell non-ODA maps and guides. Association members were commissioned to write the 'official' guides to the Path. Finally, we send a wide-ranging journal three times a year to members.

Maintenance and erosion of the Path with the attendant problem of vandalism, are constant sources of concern. We have a system of volunteers, each watching over a stretch of the route and negotiating with farmers over access etc., and local authorities over necessary maintenance; even doing minor works themselves. Since 1982 this work has been in co-operation with an 'Offa's Dyke Development Officer' (ODDO); this venture is financed by the Countryside Council for Wales and works via Powys County Council from our Knighton Centre.

We are pleased to be regarded as a body to be consulted on policy matters by national and local government and their agencies.

A strong membership and flourishing sales are the key to our public recognition and to our strength as a pressure group: please write, with S.A.E., to Offa's Dyke Association (S.W.), West Street, Knighton, Powys, Wales.

ERNIE KAY – Publications Officer

BANKS

We suggest you contact your own bank for a list of where their branches along the trail are located. Probably a Girobank account would prove to be the most convenient as there are small Post Offices in most villages.

TELEPHONES

We urge you to consider buying BT Phonecards for use in the larger towns. Life is easier when you do not have to seek change for a call box.

RIVER CROSSINGS

The walker tends to view his feet as the only certain method of progress – and why not? Unfortunately, the absolute purist would need to be an olympic-class swimmer not to have to use ferries on the South West Way. However, a certain amount of scepticism is helpful, absolute reliance on ferries is not advised!

There are other ferries available on the Path which walkers may wish to use for diversions or short cuts. We have attempted to list those directly necessary.

Tide Tables

The tide tables included in this edition refer to the times of low water at Devonport. These tables will act as a guide for those wishing to wade across the Gannel (Newquay), Gillan Creek, and the Erme and Avon (Bigbury on Sea). Please be sure to read the warnings given under each section. We have been criticized for being too cautious over the times we suggest for wading the rivers, and know that some walkers cross at other times. We believe our attitude is correct as there are certainly dangers, but you may wish to try at low tide on other occasions to see if conditions will permit a *safe* crossing. Variations in barometric pressure can affect tide levels. Remember there are different levels daily of low water, if in doubt seek local knowledge.

Newquay (The Gannel)	Deduct 30 minutes	Gillan Harbour	Deduct 15 minutes
R. Erme	As at Devonport	Bigbury/Bantham (R. Avon)	As at Devonport

* The following Tide Tables are Crown Copyright. Produced from Admiralty Tide Tables with the permission of the Controller of Her Majesty's Stationery Office.

MARCH 1994
From 27th March
add 1 Hour for BST

Days	Low Time a.m.	Low Time p.m.
1 Tu	0152	1414
2 W	0229	1451
3 Th	0307	1529
4 F	0349	1612
5 Sa	0440	1711
6 Su	0553	1849
7 M	0748	2031
8 Tu	0909	2136
9 W	1005	2227
10 Th	1052	2311
11 F	1134	2352
12 Sa	1213	—
13 Su	0028	1248
14 M	0101	1318
15 Tu	0129	1343
16 W	0154	1406
17 Th	0216	1426
18 F	0235	1445
19 Sa	0258	1513
20 Su	0335	1559
21 M	0444	1752
22 Tu	0647	1923
23 W	0803	2034
24 Th	0909	2137
25 F	1008	2232
26 Sa	1100	2322
27 Su	1148	—
28 M	0008	1233
29 Tu	0053	1316
30 W	0134	1356
31 Th	0214	1435

APRIL 1994
Add 1 Hour for BST

Days	Low Time a.m.	Low Time p.m.
1 F	0254	1515
2 Sa	0337	1559
3 Su	0427	1655
4 M	0536	1821
5 Tu	0720	2001
6 W	0840	2108
7 Th	0937	2159
8 F	1023	2243
9 Sa	1105	2323
10 Su	1142	2359
11 M	1216	—
12 Tu	0031	1246
13 W	0100	1312
14 Th	0126	1337
15 F	0150	1400
16 Sa	0214	1424
17 Su	0242	1456
18 M	0321	1544
19 Tu	0426	1709
20 W	0611	1847
21 Th	0728	2000
22 F	0835	2105
23 Sa	0936	2203
24 Su	1031	2256
25 M	1122	2345
26 Tu	1210	—
27 W	0032	1256
28 Th	0118	1340
29 F	0202	1423
30 Sa	0244	1505

MAY 1994
Add 1 Hour for BST

Days	Low Time a.m.	Low Time p.m.
1 Su	0328	1549
2 M	0416	1639
3 Tu	0515	1745
4 W	0632	1910
5 Th	0754	2024
6 F	0856	2121
7 Sa	0946	2208
8 Su	1029	2249
9 M	1107	2326
10 Tu	1142	—
11 W	—	1214
12 Th	0032	1244
13 F	0102	1314
14 Sa	0133	1344
15 Su	0204	1416
16 M	0238	1453
17 Tu	0320	1540
18 W	0416	1644
19 Th	0533	1806
20 F	0650	1922
21 Sa	0800	2031
22 Su	0904	2134
23 M	1004	2231
24 Tu	1058	2324
25 W	1150	—
26 Th	0015	1239
27 F	0104	1327
28 Sa	0150	1411
29 Su	0234	1453
30 M	0317	1534
31 Tu	0359	1617

JUNE 1994
Add 1 Hour for BST

Days	Low Time a.m.	Low Time p.m.	Days	Low Time a.m.	Low Time p.m.
1 W	0446	1706	16 Th	0401	1622
2 Th	0540	1806	17 F	0458	1727
3 F	0645	1916	18 Sa	0610	1844
4 Sa	0745	2025	19 Su	0726	1959
5 Su	0854	2122	20 M	0836	2109
6 M	0944	2209	21 Tu	0941	2212
7 Tu	1027	2251	22 W	1040	2309
8 W	1106	2330	23 Th	1135	—
9 Th	1143	—	24 F	0002	1226
10 F	0007	1221	25 Sa	0052	1314
11 Sa	0044	1258	26 Su	0138	1357
12 Su	0121	1334	27 M	0220	1436
13 M	0157	1411	28 Tu	0258	1513
14 Tu	0235	1449	29 W	0334	1549
15 W	0314	1532	30 Th	0411	1627

JULY 1994
Add 1 Hour for BST

Days	Low Time a.m.	Low Time p.m.	Days	Low Time a.m.	Low Time p.m.
1 F	0452	1713	16 Sa	0429	1655
2 Sa	0543	1811	17 Su	0532	1807
3 Su	0644	1917	18 M	0654	1934
4 M	0749	2024	19 Tu	0816	2053
5 Tu	0851	2125	20 W	0927	2201
6 W	0945	2216	21 Th	1029	2259
7 Th	1034	2303	22 F	1123	2351
8 F	1119	2346	23 Sa	1212	—
9 Sa	1202	—	24 Su	0038	1257
10 Su	0029	1244	25 M	0121	1338
11 M	0110	1324	26 Tu	0159	1414
12 Tu	0148	1402	27 W	0233	1446
13 W	0225	1439	28 Th	0304	1516
14 Th	0301	1517	29 F	0333	1546
15 F	0342	1601	30 Sa	0405	1622
			31 Su	0447	1715

AUGUST 1994

Add 1 Hour for BST

Days	Low Time a.m.	Low Time p.m.
1 M	0549	1826
2 Tu	0701	1938
3 W	0809	2045
4 Th	0911	2146
5 F	1007	2238
6 Sa	1057	2326
7 Su	1144	—
8 M	0011	1228
9 Tu	0053	1309
10 W	0132	1347
11 Th	0209	1423
12 F	0244	1500
13 Sa	0322	1542
14 Su	0405	1632
15 M	0503	1741
16 Tu	0630	1919
17 W	0807	2047
18 Th	0920	2153
19 F	1029	2247
20 Sa	1109	2335
21 Su	1154	—
22 M	0018	1236
23 Tu	0058	1314
24 W	0133	1347
25 Th	0203	1415
26 F	0230	1442
27 Sa	0254	1506
28 Su	0317	1530
29 M	0340	1603
30 Tu	0428	1736
31 W	0618	1901

SEPTEMBER 1994

Add 1 Hour for BST

Days	Low Time a.m.	Low Time p.m.
1 Th	0735	2013
2 F	0842	2117
3 Sa	0941	2213
4 Su	1033	2302
5 M	1121	2347
6 Tu	1205	—
7 W	0030	1248
8 Th	0111	1328
9 F	0150	1406
10 Sa	0226	1444
11 Su	0304	1526
12 M	0347	1616
13 Tu	0443	1725
14 W	0615	1912
15 Th	0758	2038
16 F	0908	2139
17 Sa	1002	2229
18 Su	1049	2313
19 M	1131	2353
20 Tu	1210	—
21 W	0030	1246
22 Th	0103	1317
23 F	0131	1344
24 Sa	0156	1408
25 Su	0217	1430
26 M	0234	1448
27 Tu	0255	1517
28 W	0333	1615
29 Th	0521	1825
30 F	0701	1940

OCTOBER 1994

Until 22 Oct
add 1 Hour for BST

Days	Low Time a.m.	Low Time p.m.
1 Sa	0811	2045
2 Su	0912	2143
3 M	1006	2234
4 Tu	1055	2321
5 W	1141	—
6 Th	0006	1226
7 F	0050	1309
8 Sa	0131	1351
9 Su	0211	1432
10 M	0252	1516
11 Tu	0336	1606
12 W	0431	1712
13 Th	0555	1851
14 F	0734	2014
15 Sa	0843	2114
16 Su	0937	2202
17 M	1023	2245
18 Tu	1104	2324
19 W	1142	—
20 Th	0000	1217
21 F	0032	1247
22 Sa	0100	1314
23 Su	0124	1340
24 M	0148	1404
25 Tu	0209	1427
26 W	0235	1500
27 Th	0314	1552
28 F	0418	1739
29 Sa	0618	1902
30 Su	0734	2009
31 M	0838	2110

NOVEMBER 1994

Days	Low Time a.m.	Low Time p.m.	Days	Low Time a.m.	Low Time p.m.
1 Tu	0936	2204	16 W	1034	2253
2 W	1028	2255	17 Th	1112	2329
3 Th	1118	2343	18 F	1148	—
4 F	1206	—	19 Sa	0002	1220
5 Sa	0029	1253	20 Su	0032	1250
6 Su	0015	1338	21 M	0100	1320
7 M	0159	1423	22 Tu	0129	1349
8 Tu	0242	1508	23 W	0158	1420
9 W	0327	1556	24 Th	0229	1455
10 Th	0417	1653	25 F	0308	1541
11 F	0521	1807	26 Sa	0400	1647
12 Sa	0646	1930	27 Su	0519	1814
13 Su	0803	2036	28 M	0648	1929
14 M	0902	2128	29 Tu	0801	2036
15 Tu	0951	2213	30 W	0906	2136

DECEMBER 1994

Days	Low Time a.m.	Low Time p.m.	Days	Low Time a.m.	Low Time p.m.
1 Th	1004	2232	16 F	1042	2259
2 F	1058	2324	17 Sa	1121	2335
3 Sa	1150	—	18 Su	1157	—
4 Su	0014	1240	19 M	0010	1232
5 M	0103	1328	20 Tu	0044	1307
6 Tu	0149	1414	21 W	0118	1340
7 W	0232	1457	22 Th	0151	1414
8 Th	0314	1540	23 F	0225	1449
9 F	0356	1624	24 Sa	0301	1528
10 Sa	0443	1716	25 Su	0344	1616
11 Su	0540	1820	26 M	0438	1720
12 M	0655	1935	27 Tu	0555	1844
13 Tu	0811	2042	28 W	0722	2003
14 W	0911	2135	29 Th	0838	2112
15 Th	1000	2219	30 F	0944	2214
			31 Sa	1044	2310

SUGGESTED ITINERARY

For some the fun of planning their own itinerary is a major part of the enjoyment of their holiday. If you are one of these DO NOT READ THIS SECTION.

On the other hand there are folk who have been put off tackling our path because they just could not see how to pack over 600 miles walking into a normal holiday. The answer is, of course, you cannot! Offa's Dyke or the Coast to Coast Walk, to take just a couple of examples, work out well in a fortnight. Other paths such as The South Downs or The Ridgeway conveniently occupy a week.

Our Path, we reckon, needs about seven weeks to accomplish. That being so, we have tried to divide it up sensibly into seven roughly equal sections. Obviously, if we are going to suggest weekly stages, the beginning and end of each one must have reasonable accommodation and public transport. That presents a problem in itself; so after some thought we have broken it down into six 7-day and one 6-day week. As usual, we would be very glad to hear from anyone who has tried one of our weeks and to hear their comments on it.

If you are a seasoned walker then there is a lot to be said for walking the whole path albeit at different times in our usual anticlockwise order. However, if you are not experienced, then obviously we should point out that the South Cornwall week, the fourth one in our schedule, is much the easiest if you want to start with something less demanding.

To keep the weeks set out below in a simple format the information is only an outline. IT IS ESSENTIAL TO CONSULT THE DETAIL IN THE REST OF THE GUIDE TO EFFECTIVELY PLAN YOUR HOLIDAY. Mileages can vary depending on where you actually stay! Furthermore, our mileages are only approximate because they are all "rounded".

Kilometres	Miles	Week 1 (Seven days)
		MINEHEAD B.R. Taunton W. Nat. Minehead (not Sundays or Bank Holidays). Direct coach service from London.
14	9	PORLOCK or PORLOCK WEIR
21	13	LYNMOUTH/LYNTON
21	13	COMBE MARTIN
21	13	WOOLACOMBE
28	17	BRAUNTON
18	11	INSTOW
16	10	WESTWARD HO! W. National Barnstaple/B.R. Exeter
139	86	

Kilometres	Miles	Week 2 (Seven days)
		WESTWARD HO! B.R. Exeter W. National Barnstaple
18	11	CLOVELLY
16	10	HARTLAND QUAY
22	14	BUDE
27	16	BOSCASTLE
21	13	PORT ISAAC
27	17	TREVONE
27	17	NEWQUAY B.R. Newquay
158	98	

Kilometres	Miles	Week 3 (Six days)
		NEWQUAY B.R. Newquay.
18	11	PERRANPORTH
20	13	PORTREATH
28	17	ST IVES
21	13	PENDEEN WATCH

24	15	PORTHCURNO
18	11	PENZANCE B.R. or National Coach
129	80	

Week 4 (Seven days)

		PENZANCE B.R. or National Coach
21	13	PORTHLEVEN
22	13	THE LIZARD
18	11	COVERACK
20	13	HELFORD
16	10	FALMOUTH
20	13	PORTLOE
19	12	MEVAGISSEY St Austell B.R.
		St Austell/Mevagissey Western National
136	85	

Week 5 (Seven days)

		MEVAGISSEY St Austell B.R.
		then bus service (Western National)
18	11	PAR
21	13	POLPERRO
21	13	PORTWRINKLE
21	13	PLYMOUTH (Cremyll Ferry)
22	14	WEMBURY POINT
22	14	BIGBURY ON SEA
21	13	SALCOMBE B.R. Plymouth
		W. National Kingsbridge–Salcombe
146	91	

Week 6 (Seven days)

		SALCOMBE B.R. Plymouth
		W. National Kingsbridge–Salcombe
20	13	TORCROSS
16	10	DARTMOUTH
18	11	BRIXHAM
18	11	BABBACOMBE
24	15	DAWLISH WARREN
19	12	EXMOUTH (via Topsham Ferry, see appropriate section for Starcross Ferry)
21	13	SIDMOUTH B.R. EXETER. Bus – Devon General Exeter–Sidmouth
136	85	

Week 7 (Seven days)

		SIDMOUTH B.R. Exeter
		BUS Devon General
15	9	SEATON
23	14	SEATOWN (Dorset)
19	12	ABBOTSBURY
23	14	WEYMOUTH
19	12	LULWORTH
21	13	WORTH MATRAVERS
23	14	SOUTH HAVEN POINT Ferry-Sandbanks, Hants & Dorset to Poole or Bournemouth, B.R., Western National Coach from Bournemouth to London/Cheltenham
143	88	

THE SOUTH WEST WAY

General

Tihis is a series of notes on the state of the path which we hope will help you in your walking. Obviously it is very difficult to keep something as extensive as this both up-to-date and concise. Suggestions for improvement or amendments will always be welcome. We can only keep you right up-to-date with the state of the path if YOU will keep us posted about conditions as you find them on any stretch of the path. Your fellow members will be grateful, and so will we!

If you have any complaints about ordinary maintenance or signposting on the path, please write either to the Exmoor National Park Authority or the relevant County Council, Devon, Cornwall or Dorset. They should see this is done, and what is generally not realised is that it costs them nothing to do the work, it being 100% Grant aided from Central Government for official Long Distance Footpaths such as the South West Way. If you have any major problems or difficulties we would always be glad to be advised as well.

The comments are based on the Ordnance Survey Landranger series (1:50,000 maps). These Landranger Map numbers are shown where they cover a fair stretch of each section. The reference numbers down the side are our own and are simply inserted to help quick reference in any correspondence, etc.

Towns and villages are now marked T or V respectively but the places at the end of each section appear as the first entry in the next one. We obviously stick our necks out to try and classify towns and villages. To us a town should have a reasonable range of shops, maybe even something as exotic as a laundrette! Villages should at least have a pub and a village store open all the year round, and a bus service. There are, of course, numerous other places yiou can get refreshment in season, but precious few out of it. Please note that all sections end at reasonable access points, usually having parking facilities.

Early closing days are included but these can generally be ignored in season. Places which can be reached by British Rail are also marked.

Anti-Clockwise

Information in this section is given in an anti-clockwise direction from Minehead to South Haven Point by Poole Harbour. ( ) indicates information of special interest to those walking clockwise.

THE OTHER WAY ROUND

In this book the description of the South West Way is from Minehead–Land's End–Poole. The Association has now written a description of the Trail for those walking the other way. It deals only with the path so this annual guide will be necessary for all the other information. The 'other way round' supplement is available from the membership secretary or secretary at £2.30 including postage.

Distances: Explanatory Notes

The distances shown are in four columns:

> The first column is the distance of the section to the nearest kilometre.
> The second column is the cumulative distance in kilometres.
> The third column is the distance of the section to the nearest mile.
> The fourth column is the cumulative distance in miles.

We aimed to keep the actual distances in a simple form and not pretend to a degree of accuracy that is not inherent in them. To this end we have rounded every section to the nearest kilometre or nearest mile and we have done the same to the cumulative distances.

Members will notice that our estimate of the total mileage of the route has shot up from 570 to 613 miles. We have always said it was longer than any of the authorities' ideas. With the advent of National Trail Guides, the Ordnance Survey have now made an official distance estimate – 594 miles. We have examined this figure closely. They do not include the City of Plymouth or Topsham Ferry to Exmouth. These have to be walked if one intends to cover the whole official route. Bearing in mind the whole path we feel 613 miles is nearer to the total than their 594.

The distances are of course, always marked along the Oficial Path, however bad a route it may be, unless we tell you to the contrary at the beginning of the section in the Footpath Guide.

Grading

We have now adopted a new grading system for the sections of our walk. In future each section will be graded as Easy, Moderate, Strenuous or Severe. Please note we no longer take into consideration lack of escape routes, distances from public transport, etc. It is purely a question of physical difficulty. We will try to highlight in the State of the Path sections other considerations when they apply.

We would like to underline one point; the whole of our path is certainly not easy. Some parts of it are but other parts are not. We have had a number of letters from people who have walked The Pennine Way and who have been literally amazed at the severity of some of our tougher sections! Perhaps as a further comment we may add that recently we walked two 6 mile adjacent sections. The time taken for one was 50% more than the time taken for the other. This may give additional emphasis to the importance of studying terrain if you wish to compute time.

THE TRAIL DESCRIPTION (FOLLOW THE ACORN WAYMARK)

FOOTNOTES

In certain sections we have added footnotes commenting on nine books where you may be led astray. These are as follows:

'BMG' – John Mason's Bartholomew Map and Guide Books.
'CP' – Martin Collins' two South West Way books by Cicerone Press.
'NTG' – Four National Trail Guides – published by Aurum Press in association with the Countryside Commission and the Ordnance Survey.
'AFG' – Aerofilms Guide,

| 1 | Minehead to Porlock Weir | OS 181 (T) Minehead E/C Wed. |

Grading: Official Route – Moderate Distance –   14   14   9   9
Alternative – Strenuous

The official path does not start where you would expect it to at the western end of the sea front road. Look for an inconspicuous opening between two cottages on the sea front a little to the east of the harbour.

Keen photographers please note the splendid official signs have unfortunately not been put at the start of the path. There is one on the opposite side of the road on the promenade and one 100 yards after you have started. Nonethless, if you want your picture by a sign you had better get it here. Despite their promises the Countryside Commission have still not provided one at the other end at Poole Harbour, so do not postpone your photo 'til you get there – it would be a long way to go to be disappointed.

The official route, although a good moorland walk, does not follow the traditional coastal route. Strong walkers, looking for something better, can start at the westerly end of the sea front road, proceed via Greenaleigh Farm to Burgundy Chapel and then make a steep ascent up North Hill. An easier alternative to this first piece is at Greenaleigh Farm, immediately before the house and the signpost 'To Burgundy Chapel and Beach' to fork left and then turn back, sign post 'North Hill'. This path zigzags back to pick up the official route so avoiding the steep climb after Burgundy Chapel.

When taking the steep ascent from Burgundy Chapel at the T junction go left, the path to the right goes only to a view point, and at the next junction go forward.

When you have gained the summit of North Hill, there is a sign, with the acorn, pointing forward to Selworthy and Bossington. Follow the line of this until you come to the next coast path sign, where there is a right fork marked 'Rugged Cliff Top Path to Hurlstone Point' with a yellow waymark. Ordinary walkers should proceed forward on the official route but the more adventurous can fork right and proceed working seaward by what is a well defined path.

The 'Rugged Cliff Top Path' is a splendid alternative to the official path with good views to seaward and is well marked with yellow waymarks and warning signs 'No Dogs'. At the second stile take the left fork and soon follow the rough track down by a boggy stream to the bottom of the unnamed Combe at 937 481. From here take the well-defined diagonal path leading up the hill to the wall which is the National Trust boundary. This wall can be followed towards the sea at first and then along parallel to the sea all the way to Western Brockholes. After Western Brockholes the path swings inland but is well signposted and rejoins the official path behind Hurlstone Point.

Those who have taken the official route, when reaching Bossington Hill should take the definitive right of way which goes around Hurlstone Point rather than the signposted official route. This much more spectacular and, apart from gale force conditions, is not at all unsafe despite warning signs. If you stay on the official path take care to descend the path to the left of Hurlstone Point and do not be tempted to take the more obvious path to the left (no signpost) contouring round Bossington Hill.

The official path wanders inland from Hurlstone Point via Bossington and then out to the sea again. It is usually possible, except in conditions of extreme flooding, to walk all the way along the beach, until you have passed the river, turning slightly inland there to pick up the path, so saving oneself a laborious detour. Look for the path leading down to the eastern end of the beach; the beginning of this can be found 30 yards north of a seat on the path and slightly to seaward. There is a stile within 10 yards. The beach route will save you just over half a mile walking.

(West to east continue along beach ignoring sign pointing inland.)

Please note that there is no path at all at the western end of Porlock Beach although one is shown on sheet 181 of the Ordnance Survey Map. It is fairly clear going from east to west. (Coming from Porlock Weir you go over a metal railing, which could possibly be called a stile, and down a set of stone steps onto the beach, just before you come to a signpost which points rather vaguely into space).

NTG does not mention the beach route to Porlock Weir.

---

2 | Porlock Weir to Lynmouth   OS 181 and 180

Grading: Moderate   **Distance –**   21   35   13   22

The official path leaves Porlock Weir behind the Anchor Hotel. We prefer the route in front of the Anchor Hotel which stays on the seafront a little longer, turning left at sign marked Culbone.

1991 brought bad news for this section. At Worthy you will be confronted by an Exmoor National Park notice warning walkers travelling towards Culbone Church on the official route to use the path with great care due to a further landslip possibility. You have the choice of the woodland official route or the marked diversion. It is impossible to predict this landslide. By the time you read this there could well have been one during the last winter whilst this book was at the printers. We do not agree with the National Park Authority on their choice for a future route and are pressing for a better permanent diversion when the area becomes too hazardous or when the slip occurs

You proceed from Porlock Weir by field paths to Worthy. At Worthy you go through an arch and take a woodland path up towards Culbone, going under a second low arch. Shortly afterwards you come across a diversion caused by a large landslip. You then have to follow signs to Culbone usually with red or yellow patches or waymarks in addition. You come to a bridge at Culbone running over another footpath below. Immediately after the bridge you rejoin the official path and if you wish to see the interesting church you have to turn right to go down to the churchyard. The path itself goes forward and although it is now the official path it is not always consistently marked and has not always got acorns. The sign at the beginning says 'Coast Path Lynmouth' but shortly after leaving Culbone you will find the path ahead closed because of a landslip and a diversion inland. This is well signposted along its length of 3¹/₂ miles, 'Diverted Coastpath' with waymarks first red, and then yellow. It rejoins the coast path just north of Sugarloaf Hill at a signpost marked 'Yenworthy Wood'. We believe this diversion is too long and have asked for an adjustment.

Continue to follow blue waymarks (or blue and yellow) and the Acorn symbols when you see them, and signposts: Sisters Fountain, later Wingate Combe and, of course, Lymouth.

For those who wish, there is a permissive but not definitive path which keeps closer to the coast and in our opinion is better. To take this, follow the instructions above to well beyond Culbone, you will pass Silcombe and Broomstreet Farms then turn right when you reach the second sign to Glenthorne Beach. Go down through the Pinetum and then at the second sign to the beach turn left instead of right. At the next turning right, then left just above Glenthorne House. You pass a turreted building on your left which once served as a garage and come to an unusual arch on a hairpin bend. There is a lion on top of the arch and birds on top of the turrets. There is an arrow forward to the coast path and sign on the actual signpost says Wingate Combe. Go through this arch and follow the zig-zag path up till you come to another path crossing at an angle where you turn right and you are now back on the official path. (Going eastwards after Wingate Combe signpost you proceed several hundred yards until you come to an old pedestrian gate with a blue square waymark. About 50 yards after this gate you come to a sign pointing westwards to Wingate Combe and eastwards to Culbone, County Gate. Here is an unsigned path turning off seawards and this is the alternative. It goes down in zig-zags through the unusual arch, you fork left down the drive past the garage on your right and then very soon turn right and then first left. You will then come to another junction where the left turn is signposted Glenthorne Beach but here turn right and at the next junction you will be back on the official path turning left to proceed to Culbone.)

At Caddow Combe, the official route is again signposted inland 'Countisbury 1 1/2 miles'. The sure-footed will prefer the right of way signposted 'Lighthouse' which proceeds out to the Foreland Point Lighthouse. Just before the entrance to the lighthouse where the wall commences on the right, the path takes off up the bank to the left. The beginning is clearly marked because the authorities tell you they no longer maintain the path. (Conversely, those working eastwards should go straight ahead where the coastal sign points to the right 'Lighthouse 1/2 mile'. Shortly you come to a notice which says the path ahead is no longer maintained and that is the best route.)

The National Trust have recently made a good path which can be taken down the seaward side of the main A39 coastal road so avoiding the upper reaches of Countisbury Hill. You then have a few yards on the main road but if you keep a sharp lookout you can again escape from the traffic by turning right off the road.

You come out on the foreshore. Walk along into Lynmouth crossing the footbridge, there turn right down to the seafront turning left up the steps before the cliff railway, that is assuming you are a purist and are not actually going to use the railway which you can well do if you wish! If you use the railway you do suffer slightly at the top in that you will have to walk nearly into Lynton and then out again to regain the North Walk. After all, it serves you right for not having walked the whole way!

NTG – Foreland Point Lighthouse is not open to the public.

3	Lynmouth to Combe Martin	OS 180 (T) Lynton/Lynmouth E/C Th.

Grading: Strenuous Distance – 21 56 13 35

Please note there is a long, lonely section onward from Heddon's Mouth to Combe Martin without any chance of refreshment.

The path itself out from Lynton is a Victorian idea for a coastal footpath called the North Walk and although to our modern ideas tarmac might not be the ideal footpath medium, it is a very fine high level walk indeed. This takes you very happily out to Castle Rock. Unfortunately, the official route is then on road all the way through to Woody Bay. However, there are diversions which will save you some road walking. The first takes off to the right after the turning circle (roundabout) at the end of the Valley of Rocks and then goes in a loop back, to come out by the Lodge at the beginning of Lee Abbey.

The second alternative is a left turn immediately opposite Lee Abbey which is labelled 'Woodland Walk' (each end) and rejoins the road about three-quarters of a mile further along.

This is one of the finest pieces of coastal path in North Devon and should not be missed by anyone who is reasonably sure-footed, or unless weather conditions are very bad. The path takes off just before the Woody Bay Hotel opposite the Red House and the beginning of the path is marked by a signpost on the right which says 'Public Footpath to Woody Bay Beach 3/4 mile'. This path comes out on another road where you turn up left. There will be another sign 'Footpath Hunters' Inn 2 1/4 miles'. (The sign for eastward walkers says 'Bridle Way to Woody Bay Beach'. You then walk down the road, passing on the left Hawkshill Cottage and very soon after this there is an entry marked garage 'Trees Private'; turn right here.) Returning to the westward walker, you will cross a stile with a sign 'Heddon Valley Hunters' Inn'. This is a superb path which is now the new official route. It is much nearer the coast giving splendid views. This path later descends to the floor of the valley and you should turn left along the river, signposted 'Hunters' Inn 1/2 mile', until you get to the lower of the two footbridges. Then you cross the river, and soon turn left, walk ¼ mile upstream to a gate. Turn sharp right and take a zig-zag path half way up to where the path turns seaward to wonderful views at Peter Rock. The route then takes a seaward path to East Cleave. Walkers who have been this way before will certainly appreciate the improvement in the official route from Woody Bay Hotel to East Cleave. It was always our recommended alternative route. Needless to say, whilst in the valley of Heddon's Mouth, those requiring refreshment have easy access to the Hunters' Inn.

Just west of East Cleave you will regain the old official route passing along High Cliff and North Cleave. Another of our recommendations has now been implemented. At map reference 625 482 take the short walk across open heathland to avoid the walk up to the old Trentishoe Down Road. As there are many sheep tracks by Sherrycombe we suggest you follow the grass track along the top of the combe to the inland end of it to pick up the path down.

The bottom of Sherrycombe is always boggy so on your way down watch for the way up the other side. We have seen folk so intent on trying to keep their feet dry that they lost the path. (Again, it is important to watch the route up the other side coming down to Sherrycombe from the west.)

Ascending Great Hangman from Sherrycombe, when you reach the seat keep alongside the wall on your left. There are a number of well-walked paths going out to the right but they are all wrong!

When you come to the shelter above Combe Martin, turn right on the unmarked path. This has the better views. (Leave Combe Martin through the car park, ignore path signs and go up across the grass by the cliffs.)

C.P. – The official route no longer goes to Hunters Inn and Trentishoe. See fourth paragraph above.

NTG – Page 48 shows the old route at Heddons Mouth Cleave from the valley bottom.

4 | Combe Martin to Ilfracombe Harbour   OS 180 (T) Combe Martin E/C Wed.

Grading: Moderate	Distance –	9	65	5	40

The path leaves the kiln car park and turns up Seaside Hill road above the beach. Turn right onto a narrow tarmac lane, which climbs steeply up to rejoin the main A399 road.

Walk on the slightly raised path along the road side, through two gates, then along a path at the top of the fields, to a big flight of wooden steps.

Turn left at the top onto a slip road to join the new section of the A399. Walk along the side of the road on a path, up hill for about 250 yards, turning right just past a bus shelter. Then down hill on a road to cross over the now disused section of the A399, into a lane by the side of the Sandy Cove Hotel entrance.

The A399 main road must now be followed for about a quarter of a mile until one can turn off on an unmetalled lane on the right. Further along towards Golden Cove you can take a slightly seaward path through the woods. This does give a couple of better view points but the walking really is not a great deal better. Soon the path turns off down through a field and gets back onto the coast proper for a very short distance. It then comes out into a double-fenced section alongside the main road. Where the definitive right of way, not part of the coastal path, turns off to the right before Watermouth there is now a low-tide route going along the foreshore and then up some steps. There is no signpost for the steps but they are not difficult to find, though you should be careful as the rocks can be slippery. This is not possible at high tide when one has to continue along the road with no pavement for approximately 30 yards and there is then a stile off right into the woods. The next section of the path is very pleasant on the western side of Watermouth and now happily continues out and around Widmouth Head. This new section provides some very spectacular walking; we particularly commend the view back from Widmouth Head over Watermouth, whatever the state of the tide or sea. This will be your last good view point of the dramatic setting of the Great Hangman and the Little Hangman eastwards above Combe Martin. After Widmouth Head the Coastal Footpath continues in front of the coastguard cottages going to Rillage Point.

(Walking eastwards at Watermouth one first comes to an unusual coastal path sign which points two ways. The left fork is the one to take at low tide down to the foreshore, the right fork onto the road is the one to take at high tide. If you do follow the road be careful not to turn left on the first footpath sign along because this is currently a scenic cul-de-sac. It should be part of the coastal path but it is not. The present coastal path is second on the left.)

Unfortunately, this good stretch shortly becomes a path just alongside the road but at least there is a path there now, where until very recently, one had to walk along the road. This section ends in a car park, you then have to walk along a pavement and down the lane into Hele and turn right. From there on there is a very good stretch well worth walking though inadequately signposted via Hillsborough round to Ilfracombe. This section although close to the town is surprisingly rewarding.

5 | Ilfracombe to Lee   OS 180 (T) Ilfracombe E/C Th.

Grading: Easy	Distance –	5	70	3	43

After descending Hillsborough Hill, walk along the edge of the harbour, bearing left at the slip and then right into Broad Street. At a T-junction, turn left into Capstone Road next to the Sandpiper Inn. After about 150m (170yds), turn right and walk around Capstone. Point.

Follow the coast around Wilders Mouth beach, along the promenade and in front of a parking area. Turn inland on a road, then right to climb steeply behind some gardens above the Museum. You are now in Granville Road. Pass through a gate, turn right, walk along this cliff road, before bearing right onto an unmetalled road that takes you to the Torrs Walk. It is well way marked. The National Trust have made a further small loop of coastal path just beyond the Tors whereas the official path is signposted inland and over the top of the hill. We suggest you take the National Trust path for preference for the better views it provides, they have no objections if you do.

After this, unfortunately, you come back to the old lane and the Path is taken inland down into Lee so that the fine views you might have had are denied to you. This is doubly disappointing when you realise that some of the property on your right is National Trust but it was an early acquisition and unfortunately no right of access was written into the agreement!

(Those leaving Lee eastwards should turn left up the first lane they come to after leaving the sea front.)

6 | Lee Bay to Woolacombe   OS 180 (V) Lee Bay E/C Sat.

Grading: Moderate	Distance –	7	77	5	48

We call this stretch moderate because the path is very clear and you are never very far away from an escape route. However, it does include some up and down work but is a lovely piece of path to walk.

You proceed up the road from Lee, turning right on the first footpath off it. Make sure you turn right before you reach the road after Morte Point. Apart from the two very short stretches of road near Barricane Beach, it is very good walking all the way.

(Those going east may hesitate in front of Bull Point Lighthouse. The line of the path is neither on the coast, nor it appears, going inland. However, again we have asked for improved way-marking here.)

NTG – Page 64, para 2. 200 ft not 200 metres.

7 | Woolacombe to Croyde Bay   OS 180 (T) WoolAcombe E/C Wed. and Sat.

Grading: Moderate	Distance –	8	85	5	53

This section starts rather poorly along the road south from Woolacombe and tries hard to lose itself in the enormous sand dunes. Waymarking, however, has been improved and one should not go astray. A possible alternative is to walk the Marine Drive which gives fine views. If the tide is out it is easier to walk Woolacombe Beach.

At Vention the hydrangea edged path and then the route through the car park which is unofficial is better than the official route which runs on into the road after the car park. The path climbs up through a field above the cliff to get to the top. It does not go at a lower level.

The high level path out to Baggy Point is pleasant. If the visibility is good you will get a good chance as you turn the corner to look at the path for a number of miles ahead across Bideford Bay. At Baggy Point itself, when you have turned the corner, do swing right on to the lower path. It is no further and provides much better sea views. (Going eastwards, or rather north westwards on this particular stretch, take the left fork just after you have passed the stile and the National Trust collecting box.)

---

8 | Croyde Bay to Barnstaple   OS 180 (V) Croyde E/C Wed.

Grading: Easy   Distance –   25   110   16   69

Distances are measured walking via Crow Point, White House and around Horsey Island then up through Velator to join the disused railway track which can now be followed all the way into Barnstaple.

The signs currently are not helpful at the start of Croyde Bay, proceed passing the public toilets on your right and then turn left along the beach, not easy at high tide, but do not make the mistake of coming up the first lot of rock steps at the southern end. Come up the second lot of concrete ones.

At the Saunton Sands Hotel the route crosses the road and follows the footpath round the back of the hotel and then descends to the car park. (Those walking east turn right at the top of the wooden steps.) At this point, if tide conditions are right, we suggest you walk all the way down Saunton Sands, just over 3 miles, picking up the bridle path which runs through the sand dunes behind Crow Point. After the last of the five little wooden groynes alongside the remnants of red brick constructions, you will find a gap leading into the sand dunes and immediately you will find the path consisting of wooden slats which leads directly to join the official path.

If the tide is not right or you prefer the official route then cross the car park and carry on up the minor road until you reach a footpath bearing right. You then follow a sandy track past chalets until you find yourself back on the Braunton Road!

Pass the Saunton Golf Club and in twenty yards turn right where you see a coastal path sign high up on an electric cable pole. In 100 yards turn right through a wooden gate and continue in the direction of the signpost past small hillocks to another gate and turn left. Now follow a well-marked route until you reach a sign Braunton Burrows National Nature Reserve and later when you reach the car park turn right and follow a potholed road until the estuary comes in sight and there the footpath forks left. (Walkers travelling from west to east can here cross the road and follow the wooden slatted path through the dunes to the shoreline and follow the sands to the Saunton Sands Hotel.)

When you reach the White House turn right and follow the path round the estuary side of the building and proceed along the grassy top of the sea wall. Since leaving Saunton you will have been accompanied by the roar of jet engines from aircraft taking off and landing at the nearby Chivenor Air Station and along this section you will probably find they pass just overhead on their landing approach. Follow the sea wall, past the Old Toll House and at the Velator T junction turn right along the footpath/cycle track following the old railway line to Barnstaple.

Eventually we hope they will reopen the old railway bridge across the creek in Barnstaple itself. At the present moment because of the lack of that bridge, one has to take evasive action and leave the railway through a decrepit white gate opposite the grandstand of the Barnstaple R.F.C., go up through a very narrow lane with a works on one's right and there fork right into Mill Lane. Then take the first on the right again, turning left when you come out on to Rolle Quay. If you miss this last turning you will still come up to the main road and can turn right just the same but the way we suggest is slightly more attractive.

After crossing the bridge there is a waterside walk. It is not well signed but aim to walk behind the Civic Centre and Bus Station. You will emerge by the Barnstaple Long Bridge.

OS 180 (T) Barnstaple E/C Wed. (B.Rail) (V) Instow E/C Wed. (V) Appledore E/C Wed.

Grading: Easy		Distance –	**28**	**138**	**17**	**86**

Distances are measured from Barnstaple to Westward Ho! You can avoid about 6 miles by using the ferry from Instow and walking from Appledore (to Westward Ho!) But remember the Instow to Appledore ferry is seasonal and also subject to tide, although we recommend its use when you can. What a pity that the magnificent new road bridge crossing the River Torridge has no footpath access! But it can be gained.

The old Barnstaple to Bideford railway line has now been converted for use as a footpath and cycleway and this makes level and easy walking between the two towns. After crossing the main Barnstaple Bridge pass through a mini double roundabout and you will then continue along past Shapland's Yard. You will see a sign 'Bideford Coast Path' pointing down a road on your right. Along this road you will turn right and pick up a path linking into the old railway track. The path now follows the old railway track but just before you reach the disused Yelland Power Station turn right to pass to seaward of the buildings and then follow the coast path into Instow passing along the river front to the ferry. This will add ³/₄ mile to this section.

If you cannot use the ferry continue forward to rejoin the new footpath/cycleway at the old level crossing and signal box and continue along this until you emerge into a close with sheltered flats and then keep on the road for about 200 yards to Bideford River Bridge. We would like to point out that the new high Bideford Bridge does have pavements on either side going across it and there are excellent views from it.

Leaving Bideford for Appledore proceed along the quay until forced inland passing behind the Torridge District Council Offices and the closed Bideford Shipyard. Pass under the new bridge, inland of Chircombe House and then turn right down a narrow lane to rejoin the estuary bank. Follow the footpath signs along Lower Cleave then shortly fork right and in 20 yards pass old tank traps across the path. At the next junction fork right and pass the National Trust sign 'Burrough Farm'; next turn right across stepping stones over marshy ground.

When you leave the National Trust land, turn right, signpost 'Coast Path', and descend to the bank of the estuary where a problem then arises in that there is a breach in the sea wall but if the tide is low, check it out as steps have now been put in so the breach can be crossed. However, if the tide is high a diversion has been created, so turn inland here, where there is a large metal sign 'Coast Path' with the acorn symbol. You will shortly come to a small road running inland and you turn up this and in 50 yards leave the road, turning right along the new path. At the top of the field turn right again, descending back down to the estuary where you will find more signposts turning you inland once more round the extensive premises of Appledore Shipyard. From here pass along the road past Dockside, the Bell Inn and the Glove Factory and then turn right into Myrtle Street and then left on to the Quay.

From the ferry point at Appledore there is a good 'town' walk along the front. The path past the lifeboat house is now closed due to erosion so a short walk along Torridge Road is necessary before returing to the path which ends at Hinks Boat Yard. From here, there is a road turning first right. Alternatively, if the tide is out, you can take to the shoreline just before Hinks Boat Yard and continue along the shore meeting the road you would have come on anyway.

From that point it is possible to pick up the road and go direct to Westward Ho! but the official path now crosses Appledore Bridge into the Northam Burrows Country Park. You now continue round the end of the headland, passing to seaward of the area where rubbish was once tipped in a reclamation scheme for low-lying land and then along the Pebble Ridge, passing Sandymere to reach Westward Ho!, alternatively a way marked path between the fenced off sand dunes and the golf course can be used if preferred to Pebble Ridge. If the tide is out you may be able to accomplish part of this route along the sand, but otherwise you may be diverted to a more inland path from the rubbish tip to Sandymere because of erosion repair work.

Instow/Appledore (River Torridge)	Seasonal. May to October. 7 days.
Mr Ommanney, The Seachest,	Three hours before and after high Water
Market Street, Appledore EX39 1PW.	Approximately every 15 minutes.
Tel: (0237) 476191	Tide time is about the same as Devonport.

Arrangements for parties, but not for individuals, can be made subject to tides and the normal running of the ferry for direct transport from Appledore to the southern end of Braunton Burrows near Crow Point and vice versa. Negotiations should of course be made direct with the proprietors.

NTG – The suggested alternative around East Yelland Marsh is the official route and preferable.

| **Grading: Strenuous** | | | **Distance –** | **18** | **156** | **11** | **97** |

This section is now greatly improved, our sincere thanks to all those concerned. The path begins a series of ups and downs which will escalate to become much more common and much steeper in the sections ahead; you have been warned!

The National Trust have opened a much better stretch of path forward from Gauter Pool. You no longer have to turn left there, go uphill and walk along the dreary lane with no views. Just for the record the South West Way Association asked for this.

A new route, requested by this Association, has been engineered by the Heritage Coast Service avoiding the Bideford Bay holiday complex. Leaving Bucks Mills the path climbs through woods to emerge on grassland planted with young trees. Shortly it drops into woods, within a half mile it rejoins the old path west of the old Bradgate estate house. Waymarks show the route along the top of Barton Wood into the Hobby Drive.

Once you are on the Hobby Drive, it is a pleasant easy stroll along to Clovelly. In 1991 a new path was installed by The Heritage Coast Service. Just short of the end of the Hobby Drive watch out for a path on your right. This descends through woodland into the main street of Clovelly making your visit a more circular one if you wish.

| **Grading: Moderate** | | | **Distance –** | **16** | **172** | **10** | **107** |

This is a very fine section indeed. What coastal walking is all about! Allow yourself plenty of time to really enjoy it. Whilst this section is graded moderate overall it could perhaps rate strenuous after Hartland Point.

You leave Clovelly through a large gate which now says 'Please Close All Gates and Keep to Cliff Path'. It is then well signposted for most of the route. You generally follow the fence along until you reach a fourth metal kissing gate which is of double height.

Passing through the tall kissing gate keep on keeping right, you pass an unusual summer house, Angels Wings, but when you reach an arrow pointing left and inland you have a choice. Left is the official and easy path; right are the views and you can always retrace your steps if you do not like the steep path towards the end of the diversion. Following the diversion the first set of steps on the right is a loop with some views, the third set should not be passed without exploration. They lead through a mini tunnel to a surprise view of the sea. You pass another summer house – this time on your left – stone built with a pointed green door and you come out on a platform on the cliff-top – another superb view point. From this point a very steep but not dangerous path leads down to rejoin the official path at Mouth Mill. (Those travelling west to east look for the very steep narrow path directly behind the coastpath sign pointing inland at Mouth Mill.)

There is now a good path up through the wood and a stile at the top. The path proceeds through one field and over another stile which is multistepped on the eastern side and then across another field to two stiles: at the right hand one go right, then proceed down the steps, across the bridge at the bottom, turning left, and then take the first turning on the right. This is the more sea-ward route and is now the official path. We asked for this path and are grateful to the National Trust for having provided it.

The route now continues practically on the coast all the way to Eldern Point and then on to Shipload Bay. The true coastal path from Shipload Bay to Barley Bay seaward of the radar station is now open and freely available. A vote of thanks from us goes to all those concerned, especially the Ministry of Defence who even moved their fence back to make a safe path possible. Having said that, S.W.W.A. who produce this Guide, put up the idea in the first place. If you like this bit of path, you might even care to join us! See Invitation to Membership.

Devon County Council have now stiled and signposted the first stretch from Hartland Point and Titchberry Water, the first stream you come to south of Hartland Point, has been bridged! The path down into the Smoothlands Valley and out to Damehole Point has at least been cleared and if maintenance is kept up, this wonderful part of the coastal path may be as easy on the feet as it is on the eye! Those requiring further exercise may like to walk over the cliff top on the North of the Smoothlands Valley and it does give wonderful views, but it is not the official path. We confidently recommend Damehole Point itself to the sure-footed as not only being one of the most dramatic pieces of definitive right of way in the whole country but also as an ideal picnic spot.

After crossing Abbey River, those who want the most scenic route should not turn left as directed at the next coastal path sign. Continue right out to the coast at Dyer's Lookout and then turn left up the cliff edge. It is a little further but scenically much better. Those reaching the Rocket House on the road inland to Stoke and not intending to break their journey may like to be advised that a short distance below them by footpath is the Hartland Quay Hotel which in summer operates a shop, confectionery not grocery! This is a good stopping point for refreshment and you certainly will not get such facilities again for many a mile.

NTG – Page 108, para 1. 200 ft not 200 metres.

12	Hartland Quay to Bude	OS 190

Grading: Severe	Distance –	22	194	14	121

This is a most rewarding but very tough section. It will almost surely take you longer than you think although the beginning is comparatively mild.

The path from Hartland Quay is largely track and becomes a grassy footpath behind St Catherine's Tor. There is then a climb up and down to the waterfall at Speke Mill's Mouth. In our opinion this is the most dramatic waterfall on the whole of the path and we do not forget Pentargon ahead.

The path keeps to the eastern side of the stream for about 150 yards then crosses it by a new wooden footbridge. You pass a footpath sign pointing left and turn left at the second sign 'Coastal Path'. The path now proceeds over Swansford Hill which is a great improvement over the old valley path. Be sure, going up Swansford Hill, to look back at the superb views of St Catherine's Tor, Hartland Quay and Damehole Point. Care should be taken on the section over Milford Common as erosion is making the path extremely narrow and it's a long drop into the sea.

Take care at Sandy Hole Cliff, after joining the metalled road, to watch for the signpost after about half a mile directing you to turn right to rejoin the coastal path. If you miss this you may find yourself doing about a two-mile walk down the road to Welcombe Mouth.

On the descent into Marsland Mouth look out for a little stone building, once the seaside lookout of the author, Ronald Duncan. It will provide a shelter from the elements.

As you come across the Cornish Border you will start to find a series of extremely helpful and well-thought-out posts. You might smile at the first which says "Cornwall" but thereafter not only do they point the way in each direction, but they also tell you where you are down the shank of the post. Our thanks and appreciation to whoever had this idea – surely the best yet!

The diversion to visit Morwenstow Church is worth consideration. In season refreshments are available at the old rectory.

Cornwall County Council tell us that at Lower Sharpnose the correct route has been established, waymarked and now includes two stiles.

At Steeple Point there is a tendency to keep too far inland. The official path and the most spectacular one keeps well to seaward. The stream in Combe Valley used to give problems in times of flood, but now, thanks to help from the National Trust and the Countryside Commission's new maintenance scheme, there is a new alternative route with a bridge. In normal times the best proposition is to cross the stream at the mouth across the boulders. By doing so you will miss the chance of refreshments and toilets.

At Sandy Mouth the National Trust have taken over the cafe and improved it. In season it is a welcome refreshment point, but watch the daylight as there is no electricity and the cafe surely closes at darkness at the latest. At Maer Cliff, the official path has fallen into the sea and a diversion has to be made behind the bungalow.

(Those coming over the border from Cornwall may well find they need all their training to cope with Devon's first two fierce climbs in quick succession.)

NTG – Page 110. We make it about 14 miles for this section – not 11½.

NTG – Page 111 shows incorrect route at Swansford Hill. It goes over the top as waymarked.

| 13 | Bude to Crackington Haven | | | | OS 190 (T) Bude E/C Th. |

| Grading: Strenuous | Distance – | 15 | 209 | 9 | 130 |

This section can surprise the unwary. It starts easily enough but before you have finished it, you will know in no uncertain fashion you have really had a walk! However, the walk over the Dizzard and beyond has most spectacular views, even for those who have been with us all the way from Minehead.

There are still problems at Wanson Mouth and to be fair to Cornwall County Council, even the road they ask you to use instead of the path is now liable to subsidence! Going south, the diversions are well signposted. You go onto the road just beside the stream and regain the path just behind the top of the hill before Millook Haven. (Going east, join the road just after the top of the hill, stay on it down to the bottom of the hill, the turn off is a little after the holiday flatlets on your left along a lane, **not** the slightly earlier private road.)

We are pleased to say that the small piece of coastal path missing at Cleave Farm is now available and a pleasure to walk. Those who come after will wonder why indeed such a simple piece of path took so many years of negotiation to obtain.

A superb new aligned path has been made down from Castle Point and up to Pencannow which takes out much of the sting of the old route.

NTG – Page 122 last sentence. You have another steep up and down at Aller Shoot.

NTG – Page 125 – A wrong route shown at Little Barton Strand. Follow waymarks.

BMG – Page 22 – Path just south of Wanson Mouth is on road.

| 14 | Crackington to Boscastle | | | | OS 190 (V) Crackington Haven E/C Th. |

| Grading: Strenous | Distance – | 12 | 221 | 7 | 137 |

This is a very good section, some of it tough walking, which includes the spectacular waterfall at Pentargon. The very well-graded path up to High Cliff makes the going surprisingly easy.

There is no problem in finding the way down High Cliff but you have to be careful that you are on the right path, otherwise it is difficult to get up again to Rusey Cliff. If you can see down from High Cliff, and there are days you cannot, aim for the middle one of the apparent three paths you can see. (Going east, as you come down from Rusey Cliff, take the second path off on the right.) Signing has been put in here, and the only current problem is two unsigned junctions as you get near the top of Rusey Cliff. At each of these, if unmarked, turn left. In either case, try to avoid going up to the road or down to the sea, although there is now a signpost to ensure you don't hit the latter.

This Association asked Cornwall County Council for a coastal route around Buckator and within two years they achieved it. Those who have walked here before will note the improvement.

A fine new path has now been installed from Fire Beacon Point to Pentargon.

This section includes the Pentargon Waterfall where the path has now been diverted because of landslips.

CP Dizzard Point – the path is nearer the coast than the map suggests. The variant – Fire Beacon Point to Pentargon is now the official route.

NTG – Maps on Pages 125 and 127 show the incorrect route at Buckator. Follow the field edge around.

15	Boscastle to Tintagel		OS 190 and 200 (V) Boscastle E/C Th.		

Grading: Moderate

	Distance –	8	229	5	142

A good section this, but not without some hard work. Although there are very few signposts after Bossiney Cliffs.We have asked for them to be erected.

The old spectacular path down the rocks at Rocky Valley has been circumvented with an easier path looping to the left.

Whichever way you are going, watch the footpath crossroads above Bossiney Haven. Those going west sometimes in error go down to the Beach. (Those going east sometimes go further inland than they need.)

We are often asked to recommend a short stretch of good walking easily accessible at each end for transport. We would say this is certainly such a section though we would not say it was all easy!

16	Tintagel to Port Isaac		OS 200 (T) Tintagel E/C Th.		

Grading: Severe

	Distance –	13	242	8	150

The path from Tintagel to Trebarwith Strand is again good easy walking. The stretch from Trebarwith Strand to Port Isaac is surprisingly wild and tough. This is not a section to be lightly undertaken and probably includes one of the steepest gradients on the whole of the official South West Way. Do not leave Trebarwith Strand unless you have plenty of time in hand, it will take longer than you think to reach Port Isaac.

The path from Port William has recently been greatly improved. There is an elongated 'S' bend at the start of the ascent but then indeed the path does go straight up; most of the way by a series of steps. You now have tremendous views as compensation for your efforts. When you get to the top of the steps keep by the fence and follow this around as closely as you can until you can see the descent through Backways Cove. There is an obvious path cutting back into the valley, but the more coastal one provides the easier descent. The crossing place over the stream can easily be seen but is a couple of hundred yards inland from the Cove. (Those proceeding clockwise turn left as soon as you get over the bridge and go up the other side keeping close to the cliff.)

In recent times there was a serious cliff fall at Barrett's Zawn but unless there is another, this should now present no serious problem. The path is wrongly shown at Ranie Point on the Landranger Maps. It actually goes further inland than on the map.

The Cornwall Heritage Coast has an Information Centre at The Old School Hotel, Port Isaac. Tel: Bodmin 880721.

17	Port Isaac to Polzeath		OS 200 (V) Port Isaac E/C Wed.		

Grading: Strenuous

	Distance –	14	256	9	159

There is some wonderful walking in this section and we are sure you will enjoy it. The path goes up the road from Port Isaac, passes in front of some guest houses and goes at fairly high level around Lobber Point and so down to Pine Haven. Here the newly opened path starts and is closer to the sea and more dramatic than even the old traditional coastguard path used to be. This means more ups and downs and therefore more effort, but a lot of it is exactly what a good coast path should be. The only place it really comes at all inland is to cut off part of Varley Head. The stretch around Kellan Head is particularly dramatic.

This new footpath is superb, running for two-and-a-half miles. Our only criticism of this is that there is a continuous substantial wooden fence for the whole path, topped by a line of barbed wire and we can only hope that this will mature and mellow as time goes by.

At Port Quin watch out for a new slate stile which leads onto the new coast path. Proceed on out onto the point before turning to head west.

Due to our request it could be, by the time you read this, that The National Trust will have installed an official path around Doyden Point.

There are two parallel paths at Lundy Hole. You must take the more seaward one if you wish to see the collapsed cave. The National Trust have built a low wall across its mouth which will alert you to its position.

Rumps Point is omitted from the coastal path but is an interesting diversion for those who like scenic views.

Pentire Point provides perhaps the best all round viewpoint of anywhere on the entire length of the whole South West Way; and the National Trust has recently celebrated 50 years of ownership which saved it from development.

18 | Polzeath to Padstow

OS 200 (V) Polzeath E/C Wed. (V) Rock E/C Th.

Grading: Easy   Distance –   5   261   3   162

Not a very prepossesing start to this section, in fact a most unpleasant contrast to what you have just walked before. There is however a good path all the way but do remember to see the Ferry Section. We do not recommend inland diversions, but the route behind Brae Hill via St Enodoc Church certainly has it attractions. At Daymer Bay there is a short temporary diversion for dune reclamation.

At times of very low spring tides do keep an eye on the ferry to see where it is operating to and from, as in these conditions, the ferry has to move down river and does not go to either Rock or Padstow. It may be running from just above Brae Hill to a point well below Padstow on the west side, approximately level with the red can channel marker buoy. On the ferry do remember to ask for a single fare if this is what you require; we hope this is still available to all walkers.

During 1986, the newly designated 'Saints Way' Long Distance Footpath was opened, running from Padstow to Fowey and a guide book is now available. Quite apart from being a walk in its own right, this makes a very useful link enabling walkers to undertake a circular Cornish peninsular walk of approximately 220 miles.

Rock/Padstow (River Camel)
Black Tor Ferry
Padstow Harbour Commissioners,
Harbour Office, West Quay,
Padstow, Cornwall PL28 8AQ.
Tel: Padstow (0841) 532239
Fax: (0841) 533346

Ferry operates all year, except
Sundays from November to March and
Christmas Day at intervals of 10/15 minutes.
Times 0750 hrs to 1650 hrs. Last
ferry times are extended to 1950 hrs in the
summer according to demand.
The last ferry – Rock to Padstow is
20 minutes earlier than 1650 and 1950.
There may be a reduction in service during the
middle of the day in winter but ferry will run if
required, weather permitting.
1993: Fares: £1.00 adult return, 50p child
return/bicycle.

We understand that this ferry company are no longer keen to issue single fares but we have been told that they will do so for genuine walkers on request and accordingly you should ask for a single fare if that is what you require.

Grading: Easy	Distance –	8	269	5	167

It is good, easy and spectacular walking. A useful short cut can be made across Harbour Cove at low tide. There used to be a tendency for folk to get diverted down into the old quarry before Stepper Point. This is not likely now – the upper path being better worn.

Do not miss the hole at Pepper Hole, it is only a few yards from the path, but can easily be missed. There is a post with the name on the shank to locate it.

Watch for the most spectacular Round Hole on the cliff just before Trevone. However, the path to the bottom is dangerous, and it is not recommended unless you are very sure-footed.

20	**Trevone to Porthcothan**	OS 200

Grading: Easy	Distance –	12	281	7	174

There have in recent times been minor cliff falls just beyond Trevone. Diversons have, however been suitably provided.

At Harlyn Bay, despite a definitive right of way being shown on the map, it is not possible to make progress to the west of the stream mouth except by making use of the beach for the first 370 yards.

Between Booby's Bay and Constantine Bay minor land falls have destroyed part of the original path; one again has to resort to the beach.

21	**Porthcothan to Newquay Station**	OS 200

Grading: Moderate	Distance –	15	296	10	184

Good easy walking nearly all the way. There is a little problem sometimes behind the beach at Mawgan Porth and the best route is probably over the sands when possible.

At Bedruthan Steps there is a fine National Trust car park with shop and cafe open during the Summer season from approximately early April to the end of September and welcome refreshment can be obtained here. Near Trevelgue at the nothernmost tumulus the Cornwall County Council recommend that walkers go inland following a recent fatality. The authority is unable to carry out remedial work on the seaward side of the tumulus as this is an ancient monument.

There have also been extensive works behind Griffin's Point, causing the path to be moved seaward of the route shown in some guides and indeed the O.S. Map.

From Porth to Lusty Glaze there is no coastal path – one has to come inland.

At Porth, once you have crossed the bridge by the Mermaid pub you can either walk along the beach to the post office or take the waymarked road. If you take the road, watch for a mark on the left beside a bus shelter. Go down the steps and turn right down the lower road back to the sea.

(If you go up the road from the post office, watch out for steps on your left leading to the upper road. Go up then turn right).

BMG – Does not cover total mileage through Newquay.

Grading: Moderate   Distance –   8   302   5   189

Distance is measured assuming you are able to use the official Fernpit ferry.

Please note before starting that Holywell is one of those rare places in Cornwall where you will find it difficult to find accommodation.

The main road through Newquay serves as the path. A more pleasant diversion via the old harbour is preferable to the official route, but is not available at high tide.

Gannel Crossing: the official crossing of the Gannel is from Pentire to Crantock Beach via Fernpit ferry but note this is not available in winter. At very low tide it is possible to wade the Gannel but do not attempt this except at very low tide in good conditions. Cross from below the 'e' of Pentire by spot height 58 on O.S. Sheet 200. There is an alternative ferry and two tidal bridges and an all weather, all states of the tide, all seasons road alternative. Cornwall County Council tell us that as far as they are concerned the correct crossing, when the tide permits, is to Penpol Creek where the tidal bridge has recently been extended. The shortest route is via Fern Pit Ferry which figures we use. The route via Trevemper Bridge adds 4.9 miles.

The path on the coast from Crantock to Holywell is straightforward except that it is routed through the sand-dunes behind Holywell Beach. If tide conditions are right we certainly suggest that on reaching the sand-dunes you turn down to the beach and walk along there instead. If tide and river are low there is no need to proceed into Holywell, one can cross the river near its mouth, climbing the low cliff into the next section.

(Those going north east can obviously also cross the river at the mouth and have no need to go into Holywell village. Proceed along the beach if possible, turning right to go up a sandy gully just before the cliffs start.)

Newquay/Crantock (River Gannel)   End of May to mid September
Fern Pit Cafe and Ferry   1000–1800
Proprietor – G.A. Northey   Continuous 7 day week.
Fern Pit, Riverside Crescent, Newquay TR7 1PJ
Tel: Crantock (0637) 873181

NTG – Page 35 first line. You can only use that bridge when the cafe is open.

| 23 | **Holywell to Perranporth** | OS 200 |

                                          Distance –   10   314   6   195

Grading: Moderate, but if the tide is close in and one has to use the sand dune route to get to Perranporth, it certainly becomes strenuous.

Shortly after entering the military camp area be careful not to go right out to Penhale Point (that is unless you want to get a better view of Gull Rocks).

The inland diversion at Ligger Head has now gone and apart from a short fenced section the route is now very good.

After rounding Ligger Head, when you are due North of the inner part of beach, there is a short cut down for the nimble, but we stress only for them.

They ask you to keep seaward of the white posts past the Army Camp; then the best thing to do, sea permitting, is to come down to the long beach to walk into Perranporth. However care should be taken if crossing from the dunes to the beach on Perran Sands as numerous iron spikes have become exposed, a relic of wartime defences.

24 | Perranporth to St Agnes

Grading: Moderate		Distance –	6	320	4	199

Fine high-level walking, a short section with much to offer. There have currently been some troubles with reclamation work just east of Cligga Head. This seems to give little problem walking east to west, if in doubt aim for the ruined building on the headland, after which you turn left. (Going west to east one has to watch one's route. After passing the ruined building be sure to keep on the low level path which goes diagonally down across the cliff rather than the higher level path along the top. This is not easy to describe except to say that if you look below you and there is a good clear path then you are too high!)

Some people recommend avoiding the last steep climb and descent from Trevellas Porth at the mouth of Trevellas Coombe to Trevaunce Harbour by going along the beach. Speaking from painful memory we do not recommend it – Vibrams do not grip on seaweed!

Use the definitive path up the valley rather than the waymarked tarmac route.

BMG – Path loops inland at Trevellas Porth.

25 | St Agnes to Porthtowan

Grading: Moderate		Distance –	8	328	5	204

You depart from the old mine hammerhead along the road, the path going inland of one building and then, if you get the correct path, seaward of the next. In fact a great number of people take the second inland loop but it makes little difference as one comes to the same place to climb steps to get up to a higher level on the cliff.

The walking then develops into a very fine high-level path around to Chapel Porth. Seldom does one get so much enjoyment at such a high level, for so long, from just a single climb!

The diversion on the old miners' path past the Towan Roath shaft of the Wheal Coates mine is the best bit of walking of all for the sure-footed. (Going west to east it is easy to find: go past the National Trust restored mine chimney and do not go back to a higher level until you must.) Going east to west the beginning is easy to miss; you turn right off the coast path proper between St Agnes Head and Tubby's Head. The start is a few yards after you have passed an old wall bank with concrete posts which once supported wire fencing on your left. An indistinct cross track and a middling sized grey rock on the path are the only indications. The path going west out of Chapel Porth is further inland than one would imagine. There is a seasonal small cafe at Chapel Porth.

A beach diversion is possible from Chapel Porth to Pothtowan at low tide only, but do watch that you do not get cut off. Those with time, tide and energy can go down to the beach, turn right and walk back along to under where the Towan Roath shaft is positioned on the cliffside. In this way they will see a spectacular streak of copper ore in the cliff beneath it.

BMG – Path loops inland at Porhtowan.

26 | Porthtowan to Portreath

Grading: Strenuous		Distance –	6	334	4	208

There is a good start up the cliffside to seaward of all of the buildings but the less nimble may prefer to walk up the road behind them instead.

We have reported in previous guides that the large fence at Nancekuke has been removed and rebuilt, albeit at a lesser height, and now with green plastic mesh which blends in rather better with the countryside.

Grading: Strenuous in parts   Distance –   19   353   12   220

Some surprising ups and downs on the early part of this section. There used to be hazards from roads and vehicles along the North Cliff towards Deadman's Cove but thanks to the National Trust, there is now a continuous footpath – and none of it runs along the road.

At near enough the right place the Godrevy cafe at Godrevy Towans is open all year.

Fishing Cove to Magow Rocks is pleasant coastal walking. At Magow Rocks the official path takes a diversion inland. Provided the tide and the river are low, it is better to walk across the beach towards Gwithian Towans. From Gwithian Towans the official path goes along the sand dunes but provided the tide is sufficiently far out the beach makes for better walking. You can turn up again by the two old concrete pill boxes just below Black Cliff, and these are more clearly visible than before as one of the old pill boxes now has a lifeguard hut on it which in summer has a flag flying which helps navigation.

Recently a row of large caravans have been placed above and behind the blockhouse so those, in fact, are the first things you see from a distance going along the beach. It is, however, a laborious task climbing up the soft sand to get off the beach. Therefore, if the tide is well out it is worth considering the option of staying on the beach until you are round the corner.

It is difficult to describe the route through Hayle Towans. There is a wandering route which runs roughly parallel to the sea and is inadequately waymarked.

NTG – Page 59 – map Hayle Youth Hostel is closed.

| 28 | **Hayle to St Ives** | | OS 203 (T) Hayle E/C Th. (B. Rail) (V) Lelant E/C Wed. (B. Rail) |

Grading: Moderate – No Ferry   Distance –   9   362   5   225

Distance is measured via Hayle (no ferry), The Lagoon and Lelant Station as set out below.

You have to walk inland via Hayle. There is a definitive right of way around the Lagoon in Hayle which can save some of the road walking. A track via Lelant Station again saves some main road work on the western side of the harbour. The path from Lelant Church onwards to St Ives is all easy going. The path from Lelant Church passes through the West Cornwall Golf Club course and we have had reports of a walker being struck by a golf ball. You should take great care and look out for golfers nearby. When you leave the path from the church go straight across the golf course and then pass under the railway line to pick up the coast path on the far side of the line where there is a signpost. This however is not really visible before you pass under the bridge and there is a very misleading sign put up, apparently by the golf club, which warns you to keep to the paths and rather indicates you should turn up the golf course insted of passing under the railway line. If you do this in error you come to another bridge which takes you over the railway line to the coast path but you have been exposed to danger for longer.

The seaward path at Carrack Gladden is the most rewarding; east to west try to keep as much as possible seaward of the railway line. You will probably not be on the official path but there is little serious danger that you will go very much astray in this area. (West to east route is possibly even harder to find but the same advice applies of trying to keep seaward of the railway but not going on to the beach.)

NTG – Photograph pages 56 and 57. Do not worry if you cannot recognise the picture – it is printed in reverse.

Grading: Severe   Distance –   21   383   13   238

You are now starting on the longest and most deserted stretch of coast on the whole of the South West Way. From St. Ives to Sennen Cove there is only one possible all year place of refreshment on the path and that is at the 'Weary Traveller' about 200 yards from the path along the road leading to the National Trust's beam engine at the Levant Mine. There is not even a telephone box for over 21 miles on the footpath! It is magnificent walking but do not undertake it unprepared, but there are diversions inland to Zennor, to the hotel behind Gurnard's Head or Botallack.

There used to be considerable problems of uncleared paths too in this area but the new warden service has made striking improvements. The path, in a number of places in this terrain, can be quite unusually boggy in wet weather. The problem has largely been solved by using pieces of broken paving stone and a boardwalk. The stretches behind Pen Enys Point and Porthmeor Cove can be particularly difficult after a really wet spell.

The path as a whole is much improved compared to yesteryear but we very much doubt if everyone who walks this section, walks on the correct route all the way! This is because in a number of places there are slight alternatives which may waste a little of your breath but if the weather is good, the scenery will always reward you. Be particularly careful in the area of Bosigran; a number of climbers' paths there are so well worn that it is easy to be diverted.

Grading: Moderate   Distance –   6   389   4   242

The whole of this section is very well signposted, but note first paragraph Section 29 as far as refreshments are concerned.

The official path from Pendeen Watch comes along the road before turning coastwards for the Avarack. There is a better unofficial coastal route turning off right as the road swings away from the coast just after the car park behind the lighthouse. (Travelling north, turn left at the stream in the next valley after you have passed industrial Geevor.)

At Kenidjack Castle the official route comes inland for a poor valley crossing and then goes seaward on the other side. The more adventurous will prefer the more traditional coastal route which drops down through the old mining spoil heaps and start up the other side, turning right along an old leat (watercourse). This develops into a good track, coming out on the official route near the closed hotel. Even the less adventurous can do better than the official route by following the signs down into the valley, but shortly after crossing the stream, turn right along an unsigned but walked path and you will pick up this same leat path without having to make a steep descent. (Those walking clockwise need to turn left as they ascend the road from the car park just before the high wall.)

Those who have left themselves sufficient time will enjoy the walk out onto Cape Cornwall. This was at one time considered to be the 'Land's End', when you have actually visited the present one you will be glad that Cape Cornwall has escaped its previous accolade. During the season there might be a caravan at Cape Cornwall car park from which refreshments may be obtained.

Grading: Moderate   Distance –   8   397   5   247

(There is a useful diversion which can be seen and used by those travelling south to north from Porth Nanven northwards. As you drop down the southern side of Porth Nanven look for a path going up and diagonally inland opposite you. Follow this path, take care there is a zig-zag, and you will come out presently on the broad track which is the official path.) Needless to say, once you have used it going northwards, you may be able to find it when returning south. It is not easy though, to find going southwards.

After Porth Nanven there has been a cliff fall and the path is now signposted more safely inland. The surefooted with a head for heights may prefer to keep to the old route but we certainly would not recommend it in bad light or poor conditions.

(BEFORE LEAVING SENNEN COVE READ THE NOTE AT THE BEGINNING OF SECTION 29: THE SAME OBVIOUSLY APPLIES IN REVERSE.)

32 | Sennen Cove to Porthcurno

OS 203 (V) Sennen Cove E/C Th.

Grading: Moderate	Distance –	10	407	6	253

Paths from Sennen Cove to Land's End are so ubiquitous that it is impossible to give precise directions. However, you follow the coast and your fancy until you come to the Land's End Hotel. There has been considerable publicity in the national press about footpath access to Land's End. This though in no way concerns the coastal path access from either direction, it is as freely available now as it has been for years past.

Once Land's End is behind, one of the finest stretches on the whole path opens out. The short length just before Nanjizal Cove is perhaps the best bit of a very fine section. If you are lucky to pass that way in early spring you will see that it was once a bulb growing area.

Tol-Pedn-Penwith means the holed headland of Penwith. Do not miss the hole itself which is quite close to the Coastguard Lookout. This Coastguard Lookout is also a mountain rescue post!

At Porthgwarra, if you turn down the slipway, it is possible to make a short diversion through a cave through which boats were once hauled. The official path comes slightly inland from Porthgwarra but there is an alternative path around the headland of Carn Scathe if you wish to use it.

As you approach Porthcurno you pass the Minack Theatre which most folk will consider worth a visit as it has a most dramatic setting.

By making a small detour at Porthcurno you can visit a good cafe usually open from Easter.

33 | Porthcurno to Lamorna

OS 203

Grading: Strenuous	Distance –	8	415	5	258

The first stretch is easy walking to Treryn Dinas, a diversion not to be missed by anyone who likes a scramble. The next stretch is more up and down but good walking until just beyond Porthguarnon. Around St Loy the authorities have so far failed to make the good path that is needed and one is forced onto a beach with enormous boulders, unsafe for the not so nimble. You are on boulders for about 50 metres so watch out for the opening to rejoin the path as we had a report of a walker missing this in bad weather and being caught by the incoming tide. We have asked the County Council for improvements here to take the route off the beach.

Be careful on Carn Barges not to become diverted onto the inland path to Lamorna – the better route is around the coast.

34 | Lamorna to Penzance

OS 203 (V) Mousehole E/C Wed. (V) Newlyn E/C Wed.

Grading: Strenuous and then easy	Distance –	10	425	6	264

A very fine coastal stretch is now available out from Lamorna to Carn-du, and on the beginning of Slinke Dean. Careful walking is required in parts between Carn-du and Slinke Dean. The path comes near the edge at times. The path from there to Mousehole is not so good, possibly because the authorities have ignored the old coastal route with its still extant stone stiles in favour of a sinuous new route and then a rural lane. We have again asked for an improvement of the route here as there is no longer cultivation to prevent this.

At present, the path from Mousehole to Newlyn is mostly road, but there are long term plans by the Cornwall County Council to provide a coastal path. Although it does not sound appetizing there is a better route seaward of the road along the top of a concreted drain for a considerable proportion of the way from Mousehole towards Newlyn. To pick up this drain, keep to the seaward of the buildings at the eastern end of Mousehole Harbour. When the first section of drain apparently finishes persevere by scrambling round the rocks to pick up a further section after which you have come back up to the road.

At Newlyn, pass the fish quay and cross the first little bridge over the stream and straight ahead coming out at the eastern end of the Newlyn–Penzance promenade.

BMG – Does not cover complete path or mileage through Penzance.

35	Penzance to Marazion	OS 203 (T) Penzance E/C Wed. (B. Rail)

Grading: Easy		Distance –	5	430	3	267

The path leaves Penzance by the road. Watch for the new footbridge over the railway to the path along the beach just before the Penzance Heliport.

There is firm sand to walk on if the tide is right.

The true line of the path is indistinct after crossing the new footbridge on entering Marazion. However, one can easily walk across the car parks and open spaces into town.

36	Marazion to Prussia Cove	OS 203 (V) Marazion E/C Wed.

Grading: Moderate		Distance –	6	436	4	271

There is no coastal path immediately to the east of Marazion. Before reaching Perranuthnoe there are two places where you are forced to descend to the beach but there appears to be no good reason why the path should not be reinstated on the cliff and we have asked for this to be done.

Due to storm damage and maybe, our requests, Cornwall County Council may install a cliff top path this year.4

37	Prussia Cove to Porthleven	OS 203

Grading: Moderate		Distance –	10	446	6	277

Apart from a small argument with 'development' at Praa Sands, there are no problems on this section. The walking improves from Rinsey Head onwards.

The path is now signed to go on the beach, but not signed back. However, if you do not get run down in the car park behind the beach complex, you can proceed by the official route on land.

38	Porthleven to Mullion Cove	OS 203 (V) Porthleven E/C Wed.

Grading: Moderate		Distance –	12	458	7	284

A good section this although the first mile or so from Porthleven may not impress you. There has been a recent cliff fall cutting the end of the old road out to Loe Bar and a diversion has been arranged inland through N.T. land but not signposted. We have now asked for it so it may be signposted when you get there. (The same applies the other way shortly after leaving Loe Bar you have to divert but please turn right not left!)

You walk over the shingle ridge of Loe Bar, Cornwall's biggest lake, on the left. Make for the white cross ahead and please stop and read the inscription. The old path which continued behind the cross is narrow and we would only advise its use for the nimble and packless. Instead go up the rise on the broad track 126 degrees from the cross, soon after the path levels you pass a wooden seat. 100 yards after this you fork right down to pick up the old route. If you find yourself in a double banked lane you have gone too far and missed the turn however do not despair, go on turning first right, this will also bring you back to the old path but it will take longer.

Around Gunwalloe Fishing Cove there have been a series of cliff falls in recent years but at the time of writing, they have all been circumvented and walking presents no serious problem or hazard now. At the top beyond the cove there is a stile where walking gardeners should look left. You then come out on to a stretch of road before turning right to resume the coastal footpath. (Going north, watch for the at present unmarked left turn off the road after Halzephron Cove and just BEFORE the first house.)

39 | Mullion Cove to Lizard

OS 203

Grading: Moderate	Distance –	10	468	6	290

Very spectacular, a wonderful section this, with lots of interest. It can be accomplished, too, without great effort! Unless the weather is beastly, you will certainly enjoy this stretch. If you can arrange the transport it makes a spectacular long half day excursion.

40 | Lizard to Coverack

OS 203 and 204 1 mile to (V) Lizard Town E/C Sat.

Grading: Moderate but strenuous in parts	Distance –	18	486	11	301

Perhaps we should mention one little word of warning about here. A lot of the old stone stiles, etc., are made of the local rock serpentine. This can prove quite surprisingly slippery when wet so take care of wet polished rock.

The path starts very spectacularly from The Lizard and do not miss the Lion's Den Hole early on.

Those with a taste for adventure and a resilience to scratches may like to divert down the cliff at the southern end of the Devil's Frying Pan before Cadgwith. It is then possible to go across the top of the natural arch and so down into the bottom of the pit. This is the way really to appreciate the size of this natural feature but we stress it is only for the adventurous.

It is easy to lose the path behind Kennack Sands and be particularly careful after the second beach not to get too far inland. The path, in fact, goes up the shoulder of the cliff and is closer to it than you might expect.

Care should be taken in the front of Borgwitha and behind the cliff castle Carrick Luz because the path here cuts across the neck of the peninsula and does not go down to sea level. Some people have gone astray here and better signposting has been requested.

Before Black Head there is a climb up from Downas Valley, at the top there are wandering paths through thick scrub so keep seawards as you climb and you will see the stile on the skyline indicating the coast path.

The path northwards from Black Head is now improved, a few yards beyond the coastguard hut you will cross a stile, and after 25 yards bear right along the path, leaving the field on your left. Sadly the path then swings back inland to the pig farm and after crossing the stile by the piggeries the path bears further inland. On reaching the access road to the former hotel, turn right and walk towards it. Just before the former hotel entrance, turn left at Coast Path Sign, down some steps and follow the new path to Chynhalls Point, leaving the former hotel on your right. From Chynhalls Point continue to Coverack along the lower path. The old route remains as an alternative. We suggest you walk out onto the point for good views and maybe your picnic site.

There seems no good reason why the coastal path should not continue to Chynhalls Point instead of swinging inland and we have asked for this to be provided, particularly as there is an existing footpath from Chynhalls Point to Coverack.

Grading: Moderate Distance – 20 506 13 314

The statistically minded may wish to be advised that in this section they will pass the halfway mark. For those just walking sections at random this may not matter much. To those hardier, or perhaps, we should say, foolhardy souls who are trying to walk the whole path, this is indeed a point of significance. The only thing we think we need add is that it does not matter which way you are going, there is an enormous amount of very good walking still ahead.

The path out to Lowland Point is improved but can be muddy and slippery in bad weather, though the worst boggy areas have been dealt with.

From Lowland Point to Porthoustock there has for some while been no coastal path. However, the new section through Dean Quarry has now been established as far as Godrevy Cove. The new route can be faulted but at least you have good sea views all the way. Unfortunately, the last part of this new route to Godrevy Cove has been allowed to go once more upon the beach despite the unsatisfactory nature of all the other beach sections in Cornwall! You have to aim to pass the end of the stream which runs out and disappears into the beach before turning left to come in to pick up the beginning of the path turning inland. There is in fact a signpost on the beach although this may be obscured by the tall reeds. Be certain that you find it to establish the right place to make your turn. In case this is not clear, the path off the beach starts beside the stream, but to avoid boggy ground you have to go past it and then turn back again to get to the path. In Rosenithon you need to turn right whether or not it is signposted. In Porthoustock there is a seasonal cafe.

The inland route from Godrevy Cove to Porthoustock does have one compensation, it incorporates one of the old Cornish type stiles, a forerunner of the modern cattle grid. On leaving Godrevy Cove turn right at the first road you reach. From Porthoustock to Porthallow the official route again goes inland to avoid the now unused quarries around Pencra Head and Porthkerris Point. However, we understand that locals and those who have no knowledge of exactly what a definitive path is walk through this second lot of quarries although of course they should not!

If you are a purist and wish to follow the official route exactly, be careful to take the left and not the right, fork of roads which split just after you have passed the public toilets in Porthoustock. The right fork is quicker, being all tarmac and therefore has no stinging nettles, but the left fork has more path further away from the coast.

Porthallow Point to Gillan is easy and scenic walking. The scenery then changes; walking becomes creekside rather than true coastal but its contrast of rapidly changing angles and views add to your enjoyment. We are pleased to report that the path along Gillan Creek has now been repaired and the previously advised diversion has been cancelled.

Gillan Harbour

No ferry. Can usually be waded at low tide. Predicted low water is 15 minutes earlier than shown on the Tide Table. If time is short one can proceed by road from Carne to Manaccan and then again on by road to Helford rather than walking back to the north side of the creek to St Anthony in Meneage.

We do not recommend the road short cut but the diversion around the creek does otherwise considerably add to your distance. The warnings as to variations in the height of Tide in the Rivers Erme and Avon section following, naturally apply. Crossings should be possible from one hour before Low Tide to one hour after. Please see section F.41 re possibility of an easier crossing some 200 yards further up the river.

The official route makes use of wading Gillan Creek but the distance above refers to the road around the creek which can be done when the tide is right. The way across the river is where you can go no further forward along the river and steps descend from the path to the beach. Across the river are a pair of old caravans to aim for, then turn right to pass by St Anthony's church and pick up the footpath. If the water is too deep there, you may be able to cross on some part stepping stones about 200 yards up river. This however is not the easier option that it sounds, partly because they do not go across the whole river and they are extremely slippery. If you wade, it will prove over 2 miles less.

If the tide is wrong you will have to turn along the path past two properties, the second of which is Halamana Cottage and then turn right up the lane and footpath to the main road near Gillywartha Farm House. You now proceed via Carne where you can either return along the north shore of Gillan Creek to St Anthony or, if pressed for time, take the diversion through Manaccan to Helford direct.

The path out to Dennis Head has not been properly cleared. The path along the south shore of the Helford River is permissive and is not always well maintained. Dogs are not allowed. The path becomes a track by the old railed dog enclosure. Follow this to the road and then turn right, but watch for the left turn off this road – it is easy to miss. If you come to the shore you have missed it. (Going eastwards, ignore the misleading notice at Treath.)

42	Helford to Falmouth	OS 204 (V) Helford

Grading: Moderate	Distance –	15	521	10	324

Helford to Helford Passage – use ferry. If the ferry is not running add 8$\frac{1}{2}$ miles to your walk around. On leaving Durgan going uphill on the road, do not take the first on the right as you might expect. This is a beach path. There is in fact a sign just past the junction, but it is small and sometimes hidden by vegetation.

There used to be problems both seaward of Mawnan Church and at Maenporth. These are now long past and walking is simple and easy all the way to Falmouth. The correct route, if you have the time, is to walk all around seaward Falmouth, taking in Pendennis Castle, and this certainly is a most spectacular way to do it.

Helford Passage (Helford River)
Cove Boats, Helford Passage,
Nr Falmouth. Tel: Mawnan Smith (0326) 250116

Seasonal. Good Friday/31 Oct. incl.
On request 0930 to 1730 hrs. All ferry crossings subject to tide and weather conditions permitting.

BMG – Does not cover the total mileage through Falmouth.

43	Falmouth to Place House	OS 204 (T) Falmouth E/C Wed. (B. Rail) (V) St Mawes E/C Th.

No Grading: possibly a boat crossing	Distance –	0	521	0	324

Cornwall Heritage Coast Service have been instrumental in the resumption of the St Mawes to Place ferry service. Follow the information given at the end of this section. This is seasonal so we include here a walking route between. If the ferry is not in service you can always ask. We have heard from walkers who have been lucky enough to get a lift from local boat owners.

If this fails you may be able to solve the problem by taking a taxi from St Mawes. (Take care if going from east to west, there is no telephone at Place and you should make any arrangements you consider necessary at Portscatho.) There is a bus service St Mawes to Gerrans Church so make enquiries.

If you cannot get a boat to Place House, and decide to walk the eight miles from St Mawes then this is the route which we recommend. Turn left after leaving the ferry from Falmouth and proceed along the road until you reach the castle, immediately after the castle take a left turn marked 'Footpath to St Just'. Follow this path until you come to the National Trust land 'Newton Cliff' which you enter by crossing the stile. It follows a very lovely path along the estuary with superb views across to Falmouth and the far shore. At the end of the National Trust property, signposted 'The National Trust Tregear Vean', continue for approximately another 250 yards into St Just in Roseland. At this point you come out on to a very minor tarmac road at a footpath sign 'Public Footpath St Mawes 2 miles', pointing back the way one has come.

At St Just continue along the road beside the estuary past the small boatyard and keep parallel to the shore until you come to the gate leading to the churchyard with a large sign 'Dogs on Leads Please, Consecrated Ground'. Go past the church and ignore the turning on the right marked

'Way out'. Continue forward through a lych gate, past the house 'Lanzeague' and then bear right to reach a gate with a signpost 'Public Footpath St Just Lane'. The path now continues forward following the line of the hedge and then passes through a five-barred gate and two metal gates to reach the road, where you will find on the gate pillar a sign 'Public Footpath St Just Church'. Turn left and walk along the road for about 150 yards ignoring the first footpath on the right. Immediately past a house and one more field you will reach another footpath sign on the right marked 'Public Footpath Trethen'. Take this path and when you come out on to a large field continue forward along the top edge and in the far corner of the field you will come to a stone stile with another footpath sign. Continue along the top of the next field over another stile and then round to the right along the hedge and leave by another footpath sign onto a road at Trethen. Turn right down the road to join the A3078.

At Trethen Mill turn left, this is on the bridge crossing the creek, and immediately after crossing the bridge turn right up some stone steps and up through the wood. There is no signpost here for the public footpath but we have asked for one. Ascend the wooded path to a field and cross this on bearing 110^0 to an exit by a large tree, again no signpost, but turn right here on to bearing 140^0 across the next field and leave by a wooded track. At the top of this there is a stone stile leading into a field; turn diagonally right across this to join the hedge and follow it until you reach the road. At this point there is actually the wooden post of a footpath sign with Trethen Mill on it and we have asked for this to be repaired. Turn right down the road.

At the next junction follow the road curving round to the right past Polhendra Cottage and then immediately left through a five-barred metal gate as indicated by the footpath sign. Go straight across the field descending to the far hedge where you will find a very small stone slab bridge crossing a little stream. Ascend the next field along the hedge on your left and at the top ascend some stone steps and cross the next two fields on bearing 125^0 to leave the second field over another stone stile down steps on to the road. Turn right here and with Portscatho on your left continue forward through Gerrans past Tregassick, Trewince and down the road to Froe. Shortly after passing Froe you will see a sign on the right 'Footpath to Place by Percuil River'. Leave the road by this path and cross the creek over a small wooden footbridge and then turn right back along the creek. You then follow a good path along the creek with good views of the estuary until you reach Place and pick up the coastal path with the sign 'St Anthony Head 1¼ miles' and the usual acorn symbol.

NTG – There is a St Mawes to Place ferry.

Falmouth/St Mawes
St Mawes Ferry Co.,
75 The Beacon, Falmouth, TR11 2BD.
Tel: (0326) 313813 – Nov-March
(0326) 313201 – April-Oct
(0850) 769127

All year round. Weather permitting.
Falmouth/St Mawes (Summer Service)
Weekdays: 0830 hrs, 0945 hrs, then ½ hourly to 1715 hrs. Sundays (commencing mid May) 1000 to 1700 hrs. Hourly. Depart Falmouth, Prince of Wales Pier. St Mawes/Falmouth. Weekdays 0900, 0945, then ½ hourly until 1715 hrs. Sundays (commencing mid May) 1030 to 1730 hrs. Hourly.
Nov. to March boats daily. From Falmouth 0830, 1015, 1115, 1315, 1415, 1615 hrs. From St Mawes 0900, 1045, 1145, 1345, 1445, 1645 hrs. No Sunday Service.

The St Mawes Ferry Co. are prepared to land pre-organized parties of 20 or more at Place House. To do this they would need prior knowledge to lay on an extra boat. This is also dependent on the state of the tide and weather.

St Mawes/Place House (St Anthony)
For information please write to:
Mr R Balcombe
75 Drump Road
Redruth TR15 1PR
Tel: (0209) 214901

Seasonal
Daily – 5 May–30 September
St Mawes to Place ½ hourly from 1000 to 1630 hrs. No 1300 boat. Place to St Mawes ½ hourly from 1015 to 1645. No 1315 boat.

44 | Place House to Portscatho

Grading: Easy

| Distance – | 10 | 531 | 6 | 330 |

At Place House there is an unfortunate diversion to circumnavigate, but it is good easy walking, once the coast is reached, all the way to Portscatho.

Thanks to the National Trust there is an excellent circular half-day's walk for motorists from the car park at Porth Farm. The Trust have made a path beside the creek from near Porth Farm to Place. At Place House pick up the coastal path, going round St Anthony Head, turning inland at Towan Beach to get back to Porth Farm.

45 | Portscatho to Portloe

OS 204 (V) Portscatho E/C Wed.

Grading: Strenuous

| Distance – | 12 | 543 | 7 | 337 |

Watch for an indistinctly marked path beyond Creek Stephen Point going down to beach and a diversion around the hotel before Pendower Beach. (Going east to west, be careful not to turn first left passing in front of the house by the pine trees 930 390, also watch for the path down to the beach before Creek Stephen Point just after Curgurrel Farm Harbour; this name is not on the map but a notice board currently advertises its presence.) A cliff fall near the Nare Hotel has taken away the coast path, there is a marked diversion. At low tide you could walk the beach to avoid it. This used to be a particularly difficult section to navigate but increasing use of the path hereabouts has made matters simpler. Good walking but tougher work is ahead as you approach Nare Head. Crossing Nare Head the coastal path continues along a track for about 200 yards then forks right from that track which bears inland. Just after Parc Caragloose there is a pleasant surprise for those who have walked this way before. A new, well-engineered path at an angle replaces the old, uncomfortable, almost vertical flight of steps.

46 | Portloe to East Portholland

Grading: Strenuous

| Distance – | 3 | 546 | 2 | 339 |

This stretch is rewarding and will give you enjoyment for your efforts.

As you come up from the quay at Portloe you can turn first right, scramble along and up some steps, to rejoin the coast path that way. However, the true coast path goes up the road, turns right along another road, and then shortly leaves it down some wide steps past cottages. The official route does have the advantage that it passes the Post Office which serves cream teas.

You can, if you wish, avoid the road walk from West to East Portholland by going forward behind the beach at West Portholland and walking along the sea wall between the two settlements. This does involve a minor scramble down at the Eastern end.

47 | East Portholland to Gorran Haven

Grading: Moderate

| Distance – | 11 | 557 | 6 | 345 |

The path starts along a tarmac lane from East Portholland. It turns right at the end of the tarmac to continue along the coast. The old path through the wood before Caerhayes Castle has now been obstructed and a new one made, somewhat inland. There is a seasonal cafe behind the beach in front of Caerhayes Castle.

From Hemmick Beach via the Dodman to Gorran Haven, it is all good walking: there are wonderful views from the Dodman in the right conditions. At Little Sand Cove there is a wide path cutting the corner off Pen-a-Maen Point. We do not recommend it – you will climb higher and not have such good views.

48	**Gorran Haven to Mevagissey**		OS 204 (V) Gorran Haven		
Grading: Easy		Distance –	5	562	4	349

On leaving Gorran Haven do not take the path to the beach but leave by the cliff road.

No problems provided you do not get run down by traffic between Porthmellon and Mevagissey. You can escape from the road for a little while through a kind of park on the south side of Mevagissey Harbour. (Beyond Chapel Point, going east to west keep seaward of the fence to round Turbot Point.)

49	**Mevagissey to Charlestown**		OS 204 (V) Mevagissey E/C Th. (V) Pentewan		
Grading: Strenuous		Distance –	11	573	7	356

There have been cliff falls east of Mevagissey but no serious problems currently exist. Do not leave Pentewan unrefreshed. You have a long tough sectiion ahead. At Pentewan turn right off the main road into the harbour area just after the public toilets; walk along the side of the harbour to the end of the cottages where you will see a public footpath on your left leading up through gardens to link up with the coast path behind the cottages. We have asked the Countryside Commission to make this the official path. From there on the coastal route is open although once again, with a lot more barbed wire than we like to see.

There are two bright spots in the walk – Hallane Mill Beach, a pleasant spot to picnic; and Black Head, a superb diversionary viewpoint on a clear day. This section is good exercise too, there are plenty of ups and downs. Since Black Head has been purchased by the National Trust, helped in a small way with a donation from our Association, there is a good path out to the viewpoint.

NTG – p.47 map shows incorrect route at Drennick Head. It is more seaward.

50	**Charlestown to Par**		OS 204 (V) Charlestown E/C Th.		
Grading: Easy		Distance –	6	579	4	360

The official path does not go across the dock gate at the mouth of the harbour but provided the gate is closed most people will go that way.

Despite the nearness of St Austell the path is good until near Par. You have to turn off the coast at Spit Point to come inland before the port. After the path has become double fenced take the right fork so that you spend longer on a footpath and less time on the road. Unfortunately when you get to the road there is no practical route through Par except along the road itself. Turn right along the road, pass under a bridge and turn right over a level crossing. Shortly on your left you will see the Welcome Home Inn. You should then take the second path off on the right – not way-marked but we have asked for it. In this way your surroundings may not seem as congenial as the countryside but at least you escape the main road earlier. You will also pass two cafes.

NTG – The trail described through Par is correct, the map is wrong.

Grading: Moderate   Distance –   **10**   **589**   **6**   **366**

It is a very fine easy walk out from Polmear via Polkerris around the Gribbin Head to Menabilly and so on to Fowey. Transport here makes this a very practical half day excursion with lovely views nearly all the way.

Towards the end of The Gribben there is a better route than the inland official one. If time is short by all means take it, if you are out for enjoyment and views – read on. You enter the National Trust "The Gribben" property through a big field gate. 35 yards further on there is a fork, officialdom says left, we say right. Presently you go through a small pedestrian gate. If you wish to make a closer examination of the Daymark itself and to find out when it was built and why, and even what it will cost you, perish the thought, should you wish to damage it, turn left here and go and find out. When you have done that, proceed due South and you will come to a second small pedestrian gate. The route from here is self-evident until it leaves the wood, after which you bear right down the hill to pick up the official route. If you should want the best route, but not want to go to the Daymark, after you have gone through the first small gate keep straight ahead with the fence on your right. You will come to the second small gate as mentioned above.

During 1986 the newly designated 'Saints Way' Long Distance Footpath was opened running from Padstow to Fowey and a guide book is now available. Quite apart from being a walk in its own right, this makes a very useful link enabling walkers to undertake a circular Cornish peninsular walk of approximately 220 miles.

Grading: Strenuous   Distance –   **11**   **600**   **7**   **373**

The shortest route to pick up the coastal footpath is leave the quay by the steps, starting by the public house – The Lugger Inn, turning right in the first road which is West Street. and then turning left up Battery Lane. However, should you be requiring non-alcoholic refreshment, you will probably wish to use the main street, turning right further up.

This section is very good value for money in two senses of the word. Firstly there is now a very good path all the way from Polruan to Polperro with magnificent sea views. Secondly, though, we should advise you, that it is perhaps the toughest stretch of walking on the South Cornwall coast. Those who have battled with us from Minehead may wonder what all the fuss is about but someone unused to coastal walking may well find it takes some exertion.

The better path now keeps above the Watch House after Pencarrow Point. At Lansallos Cove, at most states of the tide, ignore the coast path signs and turn right down to the beach through a narrow rock-cut cart track. Cross the back of the little cove and climb the rock-cut steps on the other side. (Those travelling Westwards along Lansallos Cliff will come across a Coastal Path Sign pointing inland uphill, and another pointing seaward "To The Beach". This is the one we suggest you take.)

Fowey/Polruan (River Fowey)
Polruan Ferry Co. Ltd,
Point House Cottage, Tower Park,
Fowey, Cornwall PL23 1JD.
Tel: Fowey (0726) 832626

All the year round. Continuous. Summer, Easter to mid October: From Town Quay, Fowey. 0700 to 2300 hrs (2330 during August). Sun: 0830 to 2300 hrs. Winter, mid October-Easter: From Whitehouse Slip, Fowey. Oct/Mar 0700 to 1900 hrs. Sundays: 0900 to 1700 hrs. No service Christmas Day, limited service Boxing and New Years Day.

In winter months when the weather deteriorates you may find that the ferry operates to and from the town quay at Fowey rather than the jetty lower down the harbour. There should be signs up to this effect.

53 | Polperro to Looe

Grading: Moderate   Distance –   8   608   5   378

No trouble here – a good bit of walking especially from Polperro to Talland Bay. Note the spectacu-larly sited war memorial. We recommend the little seasonal cafe at Talland Bay except to those faint-hearted souls who may have thought some of the coast path going was hard because at the cafe they could learn about a 10-year old walking from Lands End to John O'Groats!

In season there is a small ferry across Looe Harbour from East to West Looe. This saves the walk around by the bridge and could be particularly useful to someone not stopping in Looe but walking straight on through it. We did in fact find this ferry still running in October.

Those with time ought to visit the South East Cornwall Discovery Centre at Millpool.

54 | Looe to Portwrinkle

Grading: Moderate   Distance –   12   620   8   386

This is a section with many difficulties. You leave Looe by turning up Castle Street. Looe to Plaidy is fair, Plaidy to Millendreath and on to Bodigga mostly tarmac and of little interest. At Bodigga, the new Windsworth/Murraytown section commences. It is well worth walking despite its unfortunate beginning and end.

The official path from Seaton to Downderry is unavailable but again the road can be used, or the seawall and the beach at most states of the tide, to Downderry.

The path eastward from Downderry along Battern Cliffs starts from the elbow of the B3247 at the end of the town. It rises to the cliff top and after that the path is not at all clear on the ground because a small area of path here is still at the time of writing not yet defined. However we are hope-ful that this will soon be accomplished and then the path should be clear all the way to Portwrinkle.

We are still waiting for Cornwall County Council to establish a coast path west of Portwrinkle.

BMG – Page 76. Third line from bottom – for 'left' read 'right'.

55 | Portwrinkle to Cremyll (for Plymouth)

Grading: Moderate   Distance –   212   641   13   399

Take care when leaving Portwrinkle and do not take the first footpath to the beach but instead go a few yards further when you will see the coast path turning right opposite the golf club shop. Improvements have been made in the path and the signposting in the stretch eastwards from Portwrinkle. However, it is still not clear all the way particularly when one is proceeding from east to west. The path apparently goes across one of the golf course tees!

After Tregantle Fort, when the road runs parallel to the coast again, it is possible to walk just seaward of the road for a while without much danger to life and limb. At low tide when the range is not in use, one can walk along the beach in front of Tregantle Fort. In fact if the tide is out you can walk on the beach all the way from Portwrinkle to Polhawn Cove but the last mile is very rocky. Alternatively, provided you can pass Tregantle Fort, and that is important, there are a series of paths up from the beach along Whitsand Bay. For the record, your Association has carried on a correspon-dence for years with the Ministry of Defence to try and secure a coastal path when the range is not in use, but so far without success.

Watch for the path going seaward at the road junction to Tregonhawke as the route is complicated but now well signposted behind Polhawn Cove. There is a very good route now all out around Rame Head and Penlee Point.

Leaving Kingsand the correct, and it must be admitted the easiest way, is not simple, so read this bit carefully. On our last visit to add to one's problems, one of the Coastal Path signs was pointing quite the wrong way. The street you will walk along from Cawsand into Kingsand is called Garrett

Street, and as you come towards the end of this look for old Devon/Corn boundary mark on a house on your right. Then turn right. Ignore the sign Market Street, this time just to your left. Soon, you will approach a street called The Cleave. Just before you reach it, turn left up, believe it or not, Market Street! Now take the first on the right which is Heavitree Road (but they do not help you by not telling you that until you have walked a few yards up it). As you ascend this street you will presently see a road called Lower Row on your left. Turn right here to enter Mount Edgecumbe Park. Nearing Cremyll you will walk past a seasonal cafe at the Orangery.

Tamar Cruising and Cremyll Ferry

Cremyll Quay,
Cremyll, Torpoint,
Cornwall.
Tel: Plymouth (0752) 822105

All the year. 7 days.
Departure times are half hourly from Cremyll in summer, winter hourly.
From Stonehouse quarter past and quarter to the hour in summer, winter service quarter past only.

BMG – Page 79. Most of that road route is now off it.

---

56 Cremyll (for Plymouth) to Turnchapel

OS 201 (T) Plymouth E/C Wed. (B. Rail)

Grading: Easy	Distance –	11	652	7	406

THERE IS A WATER TAXI SERVICE OPERATING IN THIS AREA. PLEASE SEE LAST PARAGRAPH OF THIS SECTION.

For the next seven miles your walking is easy and upon concrete or tarmac in the main. You will pass scenic, historic and commercial sites. We have proposed a route to Plymouth City Council and await their response. If you are not a purist then you can walk into the City Centre 'Bus Depot and take a ride to Turnchapel. If you are, then you have to walk, so here are our suggestions.

On landing at Admirals Hard walk up the road and turn right into Cremyll Street, and continue to the massive gates of King William Yard. Pass them on your right and continue on out to Firestone Bay. At the sea wall you have a fine view to Drake's Island and beyond towards Wembury. A slight excursion could be made by turning right to walk out to Western King's Point and Devil's Point, for River Tamar views. You will have to return. From the sea wall you walk into Durnford Street, continue along it until you arrive at a church on your right, where you turn right. This short road brings you into Admiralty Street, turn left and you will soon come upon the large gates of Millbay Docks. You can walk through the docks along North Quay passing the large Brittany Ferries complex. If the gates are closed and/or guarded, thus denying access, return to Durnford Street. Turn right and walk past the Royal Marine Barracks, turning right immediately after them. This will bring you into Millbay Road where you continue on to the Dock Gates (east).

If you are lucky enough to gain access to North Quay, however, you may be luckier still and the Inner Basin could present you with the sounds, sights and activities of preparation for some long-distance yacht race.

At the corner of North and East Quays, turn right and then look for an exit from the docks into Millbay Road, where you turn right and then right again into West Hoe Road. Keep to this road passing British Telecom House. You are now in the West Hoe area and the streets surrounding you have numerous B & B establishments.

As you approach a terrace of tall houses, mainly small hotels, watch out for a path on your right known as Rusty Anchor. This is a slight diversion from the main road and provides a shore-line walk.

On regaining the main road, turn right and continue along the Hoe foreshore. You stay on this promenade all the way around The Barbican and Sutton Harbour. But, you could achieve grand views over Plymouth Sound by climbing steps opposite the swimming, pool up to the lighthouse, Smeaton's Tower, and passing that to cross The Hoe to have a look at Sir Francis Drake, still scanning the English Channel for the Armada.

Retrace your steps and continue your shore-line walk to The Barbican. A small jetty on your right is of historic significance in that it is the site of the Mayflower Steps, of great interest to our US members.

Lock gates have now been installed at this jetty, so walk on across them into Teat's Hill Road, but before doing so, if time allows, do explore the old Barbican area around Sutton Harbour. As you progress along Teat's Hill Road you will arrive at the Breakwater Inn. Turn right here, but do not walk into the scrap yard unless you want to view vehicles being broken up.

Pass the scrap yard on your right and you will see an overgrown Breakwater Hill, fringed with scrap cars. Carry on up the hill for a limestone, clifftop walk with views over the Cattewater. At a fork in the lane bear left and you will descend to the area of Cattedown Wharf. We will now just supply directions – continue on past warehouses into Maxwell Road, turn left at Oakfield Terrace Road, turn right at Elliott Road, and turn right at Cattewater Road. Within a few hundred yards you will find an extremely busy dual carriageway on your left with traffic flowing towards the City Centre. Join this road and walk against the stream of traffic across Laira Bridge over the River Plym. You have pavements to walk upon. At the first roundabout turn right into Oreston Road.

You now have a choice:-

(a) Across a piece of grass on your left you will find an old railway line which is now a cycle/walk route through to Radford Lake or,

(b) Keep on to the top of the road, bear right, then when you reach Rollis Park Road, turn right to descend to Oreston Quay. You are beside the water only for a couple of hundred yards, and at Plymstock Road turn left. Start climbing away from the estuary and at Lower Saltram turn right and carry straight on to Radford Lake.

The 'castle' through which you walk was once the lodge to a large house, now no more. Turning right after the causeway brings you to a path alongside the southern shore of Hooe Lake. At the time of writing it was not waymarked, but you should not go far wrong if you keep to this path. You will join a narrow road which leads to Hooe Lake Road.

Walk straight across the grassy area keeping to the shore and turn right along Barton Road, and by staying with this road you will come into Turnchapel.

A Water Taxi service is available to carry you anywhere you like between Kingsand, Cremyll, Sutton Harbour, Turnchapel and Fort Bovisand. Contact Tony Wilkinson, Clovelly Bay Marina, Turnchapel, Plymouth PL9 9TB. Tel: 0752 404231 or 481785.

BMG – Does not cover any of the walk from the River Tamar to Heybrook Bay. We think you ought to walk it all, especially Plymouth Hoe and the Barbican area.

NTG – Also does not supply walking instructions for this 7 miles of the coast path.

57	Turnchapel to Wembury (Warren Point)			OS 201

Grading: Easy	Distance –	11	663	7	413

Considering how close this section is to Plymouth it is surprisingly pleasant and well worth walking. It is too, a useful short day's walk which may be accomplished by catching a bus from Plymouth to Knighton, walking out to Warren Point and then walking clockwise to Turnchapel or of course, vice versa.

The good views start at Jenny Cliff and are very rewarding indeed from Staddon Heights. You look back to Plymouth itself and The Hoe, across the Sound to Cornwall and presently are able to look at the Breakwater sideways on.

Unfortunately, there have been lots of problems over the years, trying to keep the path on Staddon Heights and down the steps to Bovisand clear. Leaving Heybrook Bay watch for the turning off right onto the Coast Path after the last house. The obvious track up the hill is not the right way. Walkers on the South West Path can now find out about firing times on the range at Wembury Point near Plymouth, Devon, by calling free on 0800 833608.

The naval gunnery school, HMS CAMBRIDGE, fires close range (20 and 30 mm calibre) and medium range (4.5 inch calibre) guns out to sea at floating and airborne targets.

The coastal path passes between the school and sea. When red flags are flying, and red warning discs showing, the guns are likely to fire and walkers should take the signposted inland diversion.

Firing usually takes place weekdays, between 9 am and 6 pm; rarely at night or over weekends and bank holidays. The school is closed over Christmas, Easter and for three weeks in August. Do not loiter along the section seaward of the guns.

If the ferry is not running the obvious way forward is to walk back to Knighton and to catch a bus either to Plymstock or Plymouth itself, then a bus to Noss Mayo. Those who reach the ferry point and wish to go to Knighton need not go back up the track they came down. You return up the actual ferry steps, turn right for a few yards, then a narrow path comes steeply down at an acute angle. This is the path you want; if you continue on the broad contoured path it becomes private. The steep zig-zag path has grand views to compensate for the effort required and brings you back to the Rocket House at the top of the track. Beside the Rocket House a big gate leads to a track through a field which becomes a road. At Wembury House a stile leads to a field and to a footpath junction. The path you want is the one to the right which runs along beside the high wall. You follow this path to the end of the wall, where it goes through two successive kissing gates. It then bears left approximately 333° across fields towards Knighton. As you leave the fields it goes down a few steps. Turn left here and then first right. This will bring you out on the road. Then turn left and the bus stop is a little further down on the opposite side of the road, just before the pub. The distance back from the ferry point to the bus stop is 1 1/2 miles.

For those who contemplate walking around the estuary take care as the section of the A379 you must walk is very busy.

AFG – The inland alternative route is incorrect – it is around HMS Cambridge, not through it.

| 58 | **Wembury (Warren Point) to Bigbury-on-Sea** | | | OS 201 and 202 |

| **Grading: Starts easy but becomes strenuous** | Distance – | 22 | 685 | 14 | 427 |

At Knighton there is an hourly bus service to Plymstock and Plymouth where you can use an infrequent service to Newton Ferrers/Noss Mayo.

This is a scenic but in parts tough section. It starts from the ferry landing on the Yealm, pronounced "Yam", south of Noss Mayo. It then, unusually for the the coastal path, but nonetheless rewardingly, follows a one-time carriage drive for several miles. This means the walking at first is well graded with no fierce ups and downs.

Unusually, too, there is a definitive footpath loop seaward of the coastal path to Stoke beach; use this if you wish to see the historic St Peter's Church, but you do unfortunately get the worst of the caravans as well.

You depart from the carriage drive at the ruined tea house and then the normal up and down work starts again. St Anchorite's Rock is good for a scramble and you pass Bugle Hole, a very pleasant spot.

The new coastal section at Mothecombe then begins giving superb views of the mouth of the Erme. It has been fairly described as England's most unspoilt river mouth.

Should you arrive at the River Erme at a time that promises a very long wait for low tide to enable you to wade across then there is an inland alternative. This alternative is of about 7 miles with fairly steep up and down country lanes. You are the best judge of your rate of travel so the decision to wait for the tide or continue walking is yours.

If you follow the riverside paths shown on OS map 202 you will be trespassing on a private estate so follow the narrow country lanes to Holbeton village. Then continue on a northerly route to Ford and Hole Farm. Soon after passing Hole Farm take off on a public footpath on your right. From here to the main A379 road is about 3/4 mile. Turn right to cross the River Erme at Sequer's Bridge. Stay on the A379 for about 1/2 mile but take care as this is an extremely busy road. You will see a road on your right signposted to Orcheton. Follow this road south towards the village of Kingston but before you reach that village you will see road signs to Wonwell Beach. Just before the slipway on to the sands you have a choice. If the tide now permits you can continue south along the beach or take to the waymarked coast path in the woodlands on your left. We think this preferable because of the lovely views you will get of the Erme Estuary.

For those walking west: do not follow riverside tracks shown on OS map but take the road inland and uphill towards Torr Down and at Great Torr turn left to Orcheton and the A379. Turn left on the A379 for 1/2 mile. You will pass the large gates of the Flete Estate and about 300 yards past these you will see a rough lane on your left. This is a public footpath through to Hole Farm where you will join the tarmac lane to Ford and Holbeton village. Keep to the country lanes to Mothecombe. After a steep descent towards the beach and before you reach it you will see the coast path sign on your right.

Beyond the Erme the walking becomes tougher, but the views forward, and back, provide compensation.

If the tide is very low you could go onto Westcombe Beach and walk on to Ayrmer Cove via caves that lead from one beach to the other. You have a choice of two, both being about 15 yards long. You will walk on shingle through them, but be a little careful on rocks that can be slippery once you have reached Ayrmer Cove.

The River Yealm ferry has stopped operations. Other than a tedious and often busy road walk your method of crossing this estuary is by bus from Wembury (or Noss Mayo).

Reasonably priced taxis are available:–

Kev's Cabs – 0752 872367 and

Tim's Taxis – 0752 830225

If the ferry closure becomes permanent we have asked the Countryside Commission to explore the possibility of creating an estuary walk around the River Yealm.

The Heritage Coast Service is trying very hard to establish a ferry service and by the time you read this there may be one. A phone call to 0803 861234 might be of assistance.

River Erme   No ferry.

Low water is at about the same time as the Devonport Tide Table shown here.

It is usually possible to wade the river 1 hour each side of low water along the old ford. Great care should be taken because heavy rains or seas can make the crossing dangerous. On modern maps the old ford is not shown but this in fact ran from Ordnance map ref. 614 476 to map ref. 620 478. In other words, the old ford connected the road by the row of coastguard cottages with the end of the inland road to Wonwell Beach from Kingston.

BMG – Page 16. Go further upstream to wade the Erme – Cross towards the road on the east side. Woodland route not shown from that road southwards.

| 59 | **Bigbury-on-Sea to Hope Cove, Inner Hope** | OS 202 (V) Bantham (V) Thurlestone E/C Th. |

Grading: Moderate   Distance –   9   694   6   433

This is an easy section, unfortunately parts of it are overcrowded in season. The easy route from Bigbury to the ferry at low tide only, is over the sands, along the west bank of the River Avon. However, the short cut does not have as good views as the longer official route.

The official route turns right at the bottom of the road on to what is called Clematon Hill at the western side of the mouth of the River Avon. This particular piece of path is of sentimental interest to the South West Way Association being the first practical improvement in the routing of the path which was accepted and became part of the official path.

There are good views here across the estuary but unfortunately you have to walk up the busy road to Mount Folly Farm afterwards. However, again there is compensation because the views southward across the estuary just after the farm are particularly spectacular.

There were recent problems at Thurlestone Golf Course but these have been resolved and the path is happily back on the coast once more. However, you should take great care where the path proceeds along the seaward boundary of the Thurlestone Golf Course, watching out for golfers and where they hit the ball. We have had a report of a walker on this section who was hit in the mouth by a golf ball at close range with resulting horrific damage to teeth and lips.

Bigbury/Bantham (River Avon)
H. Cater, Yorick, West Buckland,
Kingsbridge, Devon.
Tel: Kingsbridge (0548) 560593.

Seasonal. Easter 2 weeks, then mid-May to
end August Mon. to Sat. 1000 to 1100 hrs,
1500 to 1600 hrs.
No Sunday service.

We suggest you telephone Mr Cater day before you require the ferry and give him your estimated time of arrival.

Low water is at about the same time as the Devonport Tide Table.

Please note when the ferry is not running then a recommended way to reach Bantham is by taxi (Arrow Cars – 0548 856120 or D & C Taxi – 0548 561560). It is possible at low tide, when not rough, or the river is not in flood, to wade the river. However, we strongly stress we are not advising this as a cheap method of avoiding the ferry crossing. When the ferry is working, you are strongly advised to use it because wading is not easy and you may get a lot wetter than you expect. You will most likely be up to your thighs in water and in no circumstances should the crossing be attempted if conditions are wrong. The two guide points are just below the ferry crossing. On the true right bank – the western side – there is a well defined hedge running North and South with pine trees. On the left bank – the eastern side – there is a castellated building with battlements and a little flag pole in the middle. (This castle is just above the famous thatched boat house which is so well known from many pictures taken of the River Avon and Bantham.) However, if crossing from the true right to the left – in other words from west to east – take off at the hedge and wade towards the castle-like building. If going the other way, vice versa. Please note it is important that you do wade at this point. The river looks shallow in a number of other places but there are deeper channels and indeed soft sand patches which can make it extremely difficult. Further towards the sea, there is a considerable tidal ebb which can be exceedingly dangerous.

It should always be borne in mind that the depth of water at low tide and consequently safe passage across is affected by natural conditions inasmuch that strong south west or westerly winds tend to bank up water in the English Channel and that therefore, there will be a greater depth of water than expected. This will also happen if there is a lot of rain in the catchment areas of the rivers, with consequently more water coming down. Caution: although we know several who have waded the River Avon we do not recommend it; great care is required, especially by those with backpacks.

VERY IMPORTANT – PLEASE TAKE NOTE

AT DEAD LOW WATER WE STRESS THAT YOU MUST CONSIDER VERY SERIOUSLY WHETHER YOU SHOULD WADE THIS RIVER. IT IS VERY DIFFICULT AND CAN BE DANGEROUS EVEN FOR TALL AND STRONG ADULTS. MANY OF OUR MEMBERS, INCLUDING YOUR SECRETARY WILL NOT VENTURE ACROSS. THEIR OPINION BEING – 'WHEN THE FERRY IS NOT RUNNING THEN THE ONLY ALTERNATIVE IS TO GO ROUND'.

INLAND WALKING ROUTE

There are riverside footpaths along both west and east banks of the River Avon to Aveton Gifford. This makes the inland walking route from Bigbury-on-Sea to Bantham and vice versa about 9 miles in total. The O.S. Landranger Series 2 maps show the riverside paths. What you have to watch is that the road, between the words 'ford' is tidal so is at times submerged.

60	Hope Cove, Inner Hope to Salcombe, Ferry	OS 202 (V) Hope Cove E/C Wed.

Grading: Strenuous		Distance –	12	706	7	440

Excellent coastal walking, some of the finest in South Devon. This section also makes an easily accomplished day walk from Kingsbridge or Marlborough using Hope and Salcombe buses.

AFG – Incorrect route shown between Soar Mill Cove and Bolt Head.

BMG – Incorrect route shown between Soar Mill Cove and Off Cove.

61 | Salcombe to Torcross

OS 202 (T) Salcombe E/C Th. (V) Beesands

Grading: Strenuous Distance – 20 726 13 453

This has always been first class walking but in time past it has sometimes been marred by poor clearance. A lot of work has recently been done so that we do not think you will now have real trouble anywhere.

Be sure to keep to the lower coastal path around Rickham Common, this is much the better route.

Always try to leave yourself enough time on this section to make the diversion down to the old deserted village at Hall Sands. Very few who go down there and see the ruins right beside the sea will not be moved by the experience. The cliff continues to slip at the existing village and the path has been diverted inland of the buildings over a 200 yard stretch.

Those who do not mind a trudge along the pebbles can, at low tide, walk along the beach from Sunnydale to Torcross; there is a little inland diversion you can make here into the old slate quarry through a cart-track cutting in the rock. The official path goes up inland behind this disused quarry.

(Travelling west go to seaward of the Torcross Hotel, the path starts right on the sea front.)

Salcombe/E. Portlemouth
The Salcombe Ferry Operating Co. Ltd.
North Lodge, Landmark Road, Salcombe,
Tel: Salcombe (0548) 842061/842364

All year round Nov.-March.
0800 to 1700 hrs half-hourly. April-October continuous service running to 1930 hrs.
July and August Sundays, Saturdays and Bank Holidays 0830 hrs start.

NTG – Page 110 paragraph 5. The accommodation is only self-catering apartments.

62 | Torcross to Dartmouth

OS 202 (V) Torcross E/C Sat. (V) Strete E/C Wed. (V) Stoke Fleming E/C Th.

Grading: Moderate Distance – 16 742 10 463

There is no coastal path currently available from Strete Gate to beyond Redlap Cove; plans are afoot for an improved route from Stoke Fleming onwards but there is still a lot to be done before that is achieved.

Thanks to the Women's Institute and the National Trust, a good coastal path is available from beyond Redlap as far as Dartmouth Castle. This short section at least shows you how good the coastal walking will be around here when the coastal route is complete.

An excellent half-day circuit here, park at Dartmouth Castle proceed up the private road but public path via the Coastguard cottages and on to Little Dartmouth. Here turn seaward over the stile just before the car park and return by the coastal path to Dartmouth Castle; there is even a bridge over the sea to interest the youngsters!

At certain times of the year there is a ferry service between the Castle and Dartmouth. You could have a nice boat trip and avoid street walking.

NTG – Page 117 – map, no Youth Hostel at Strete now.

BMG – The route shown between Strete Gate and Stoke Fleming is not the official one – see NTG. But this poor route could be altered soon by Devon County Council. Hopefully for a better one but we are not very optimistic

BMG – The better route to Dartmouth Castle is not shown.

Grading: Strenuous	Distance –	18	760	11	474

Much of the new path is on the estate owned by the late Lt Col Jones, the Falkland Islands V.C., and has very properly been dedicated to his memory. It is interesting to know that the little battlemented tower you pass at Mill Bay Cove was in fact a mill.

There are regular ferries across the Dart which run all the year. The lower ferry is the one walkers will normally take and just beyond the top of the slipway there is an arch through which one can turn right and then left up the steps then right along the path which comes to a minor road, keep right along this turning off on the footpath just above Mill Bay Cove. The path goes down to the Cove and then takes a small inland loop behind two houses and then gets back to the coast and stays on it all the way to nearly Crab Rock Point.

The South West Way Association has been responsible for a minor improvement just before Berry Head. The path now stays a little longer on the coast and then turns only slightly inland to go on a path behind the fort and not onto the road as it used to do. The more agile, though, may prefer simply to keep seaward of the fort by scrambling down the wall of the ditch.

There is a cafe which you could easily miss actually inside the main Berry Head Fort, which is the second fort that you come to. This cafe, as well as opening in season, is sometimes open out of season as well.

Having left Berry Head you will follow Berry Head Road and when you reach the Breakwater descend to the new promenade which follows the water's edge, past the new marina, to the inner harbour.

Dartmouth/Kingswear
South Hams District Council, Lower Ferry,
Lower Ferry Office, The Square,
Kingswear TQ6 0AA
Tel: (0803) 752342

0700/2255 hrs Sunday start 0800 hrs.
Winter – 10 minutes service, Summer
– 6 minutes service.
Last ferry leaves: Dartmouth 2255 hrs,
Kingswear 2245 hrs.

Though walkers will normally use the lower ferry, if by chance this is not running then there is a passenger ferry usually operating further up the river, with the higher ferry beyond this.

Grading: Moderate	Distance –	13	773	8	482

Distances are taken along the official path where there is one, then along the back of Goodrington Sands beach, around Roundham Head, along Paignton and Preston sea fronts and along the promenade at Torquay.

The path is fair from Brixham to Elbury Cove though not as scenic as one might hope. From Elbury Cove to Goodrington, it deteriorates and becomes more urbanised. Beyond that, the official path becomes more of a promenade than a path and is mostly urban walking. Having said that, there are lots of worse bits on the path so by all means quicken your step, especially in season, but do not dread too much!

When departing from Brixham it is no longer necessary to leave the inner harbour by the dangerous Overgang Road but instead take the new path signposted "Coastal Footpath to Oxen Cove and Freshwater Car Park". At the car park continue on past the Zeneca Brixham Environmental Laboratory and on to the Battery Gardens where you follow the lower path to Fishcombe Cove where a new sign shows the way.

At the end of Elbury Cove leave the beach by ascending the steps. Take care at Broadsands beach that you do not follow the path up the cliff at the eastern end but turn left and proceed a few yards up the road under the bridge and then turn immediately right where the coastal path is signposted.

At Hollicombe Head you can turn right and go through the delightful park that was once the gas works. Bear left to emerge through the main gate onto the road.

CP – Between Broadsands and Goodrington the path crosses back under the railway line. There is no road walking until Paignton Harbour.

NTG – Page 133. Do not use Overgang. Look out for new coast path.

NTG – Broadsands – stay with the sea wall until well past halfway.

BMG – Does not cover Brixham to Babbacombe. Over ten miles omitted!

---

65 | Torquay Harbour to Shaldon

OS 202 (T) Torquay E/C Wed. (B. Rail)

Grading: Strenuous   Distance –   17   790   11   493

You walk round the back of Torquay Inner Harbour turning left up Beacon Hill. You soon come alongside a massive hotel. The Imperial, and turn sharp right passing across the front of its palatial front doors. Watch for this right turn there are often so many vehicles here they obscure the sign. Just before the path becomes a dead end you turn left up steps, though it is worth going the few extra yards to have the best view of the Natural Arch or London Bridge as it is often called. You now have a surprisingly energetic and scenic little stretch coming out on a grassy plateau called Daddyhole Plain. Turn right passing through the car park area to find the path at the other side going East, to Meadfoot Beach. Go along by Meadfoot beach bearing right at the end through another little car park to go up and join the Marine Drive, turning right just before you come opposite to Thatcher Rock.

On the road by the car park above Ansteys Cove you can, time and energy permitting, follow an interesting and enjoyable route down the path to Ansteys Cove, around to Redgate Beach and then rejoin the official path at Walls Hill.

At Oddicombe it is important that after you have gone under the cliff railway you turn right this means going downwards at the start. We state this because N.T.G. says 'going up and down' which is misleading.

West of Maidencombe we are pleased to say there is a further improvement in fact one we suggested over ten years ago! After Watcombe you ascend a steep uphill with a handrail, locally known as the Goat Path. At the top you now turn right into the wood and the route is then coastal all the way to Maidencombe coming out in the car park above the beach. From the car park you go a few yards up the road and turn right. That is unless you wish to visit the seasonal cafe in that case you will have to go a little further up the road and then come back and turn left. Whatever you did there, shortly after you have restarted the coastal path there is a sharp left and then a right turn before you come to the last house.

There have been improvements on the route to Labrador but there are still some stiff gradients so be prepared for these. The path brings you out alongside the main road. Turn right here along the pavement, shortly there is sunken path beside the road which comes to the main road again by a drive entry. Just beyond this is a stile by a field gate, enter. There are superb views as you descend but ensure you keep to the bottom edge of the pitch and putt where you will pick up the path going down steps. Follow the path around The Ness.

NTG – Page 139. Paragraph 3 states 'after railway up and down'. In fact it is 'down and up'.

NTG – Page 141. The route shown between Valley of Rocks and Bell Rock is 'incorrect.

---

66 | Shaldon to Exmouth via Topsham Ferry

OS 192 (V) Shaldon E/C Th. (T) Teignmouth E/C Th. (B. Rail) (T) Dawlish E/C th. (B. Rail)
(V) Dawlish Warren E/C Th. (B. Rail) (V) Stracross E/C Th. (B. Rail)

Grading: Easy   Distance –   30   820   19   512

Distance is measured by diverting inland to the main road at Holcombe and then along to the centre of Dawlish. It also includes the diversion inland to use the ferry at Topsham.

We are pleased to say that there has now been some improvement to this section of the path, although from Smugglers Lane to Windward Lane the path continues as before over the existing section of the A379 for approximately 150 metres. The path then turns right away from the main road, along the hedge to the cliff edge, and then crosses two fields before turning left to emerge via steps onto the road again near the Old Teignmouth Road. Unfortunately, part of this section is still on the main road requiring a double crossing of the road as the only pavement is on the far side. To walk the new section do take care to turn into Derncleugh Gardens and then follow the signs as it is possible to miss them on the main road.

From Dawlish it is possible at low tide to walk along the sea wall to Dawlish Warren. At high tide, one can walk part way along in front of the railway station and then turn inland over a footbridge. There is a short stretch of official path from the point where the main road turns inland via Langstone Rock to Dawlish Warren. There is again no official path along Dawlish Warren as originally envisaged but it is a good walk none the less. At present in summer one must walk inland to Starcross to get the ferry to Exmouth. In winter this ferry does not run so that you have three alternatives, you can catch a train at Dawlish Warren or Starcross changing at Exeter and going back down to Exmouth. You can do approximately the same thing by bus changing over routes either at Countess Wear or in Exeter, whichever you prefer, and again going back to Exmouth. The purist though – and what are a few more miles after all the ones we have travelled? – can walk round to Exmouth by using the year-round ferry at Topsham (see ferry section and details in paragraph below).

Walk north from Starcross forking right to leave the A379 to proceed northwards to Powderham Church. Here a footpath goes forward at first on the estuary bank and then on the canal footpath up to the ferry point opposite Topsham. Here you can cross over using the ferry, then, unfortunately, you have to go out on the main road by crossing the level crossing and proceeding out towards Clyst St. George. About half a mile from Clyst Bridge turn right on a footpath and follow that to Ebford. You eliminate over half a mile of main road walking. Turn south along the A377 but turn right off it just prior to the junction of the A377 with the B3281 and go into Lympstone. Lympstone is a pleasant old world village and from there south there is a riverside footpath all the way down to Exmouth. Admittedly when last used it was not in as good repair as it should have been, but we have made representations about it, so that we hope it is now improved.

(We have heard of walkers being fortunate enough to obtain a passage on small boats at Exmouth across to Dawlish Warren. If anyone is fortunate enough to use this service we hope they will recompense those responsible well so that others following will also be as lucky.) However, with the advent of Exmouth Water Taxis the sandy nature reserve can now be walked all the way.

Shaldon/Teignmouth (River Teign)
Teignbridge District Council, Resort Managers Office, Forde House, Newton Abbot, TQ12 4XX. Tel: Teignmouth (0626) 779770 Resort Manager or (0626) 779769 Tourist Information Centre

All year round. 20 minutes service. Easter to November 7 days a week 0800–dusk. January to Easter, Monday to Friday only 0800–1700.

Starcross/Exmouth (River Exe)
Mr B Rackley,
Starcross Pier & Pleasure Company,
26 Marine Parade,
Dawlish.
Tel: (0626) 862452

From Starcross Pier. Seasonal. 7 days a week. 1 May-15 October. 1000 hrs then every hour on the hour, last ferry 1745 hrs. From Exmouth, Ferry Steps. 1030 hrs, then every hour on the half hour, last ferry 1815 hrs. Crossing approx. 15 minutes.

In winter and at other times when the ferry is not running, it is possible to catch a train from Dawlish Warren, changing at Exeter and going to Exmouth or to catch a bus at Exeter and cross over at Countess Wear and catch a bus to Exmouth.

A preferable alternative is to make use of a new venture called Exe Water Taxis. They will pick up and drop passengers on the tip of Dawlish Warren. No more road walking via Starcross. Contact: Bob or Jenny Killick, 60 High Street, Topsham, EX3 0DY (0392 873409).

Topsham Ferry (River Exe)
Exeter City Council Canals & Rivers Dept.
Tel: Exeter 74306.

All year round 6 days a week. Oct./April 0800-1730 hrs. May/Sept. 0800-2000 hrs. Intervals between runs as demand occasions. Closed all day Tuesday. Dependent on tide and weather.

BMG – Page 29. The official path goes up and onto the point west of Shaldon – see NTG

BMG – Page 31. When Starcross Ferry not running you need not go into Exeter – use Topsham Ferry – as above.

67 | Exmouth to Budleigh Salterton

Grading: Moderate	Distance –	10	830	6	518

No real problems here for walkers but keep inland of the range at Straight Point.

68 | Budleigh Salterton to Sidmouth

Grading: Starts moderate but becomes strenuous	Distance –	11	841	7	525

The start is along a raised path inland to the River Bridge at South Farm, then a riverside path back to the coast.

The path around High Peak is well marked but it does not unfortunately go over the top as you, and many others in the past, obviously expected. If you do battle your way to the top you will certainly not be disappointed with the views. The path on the top of Peak Hill immediately west of Sidmouth has been improved to give better seaward views.

The descent from Peak Hill towards Sidmouth takes you down through a wood and out on to the road. Cross the road into a field where a newly created path will separate you from busy traffic. You leave the field to cross the road again to parkland for the descent into Sidmouth. Later, flower lovers will prefer the longer route through the Connaught Gardens, but you have to come back to the road in the end.

69 | Sidmouth to Seaton

Grading: Strenuous	Distance –	15	856	9	534

Please note that there are a number of quite considerable ascents and descents on this section. Do not judge the effort required purely on the mileage. There are one or two places in this stretch where it is easy to come off the route but one is not likely to come to any severe harm.

After Branscombe Mouth there are alternative paths. The one over Hooken Cliffs gives superb views and is probably easier to walk. The undercliff path, apart from the beginning among the caravans is scenically better and we would recommend this if the weather is good. You have the interesting undercliff itself, the massive cliffs to the left, interesting rock formations ahead, and good views to seaward.

At most states of the tide it is possible to walk along the beach from Seaton Hole to Seaton, avoiding some road work. (If leaving Seaton at low tide keep along the promenade and then walk along the beach to Seaton Hole, turning up the path there to come back, briefly, to the road.)

WATCH THE TIDE – YOU CAN GET CUT OFF.

CP – The path is nearer the coast than the map suggests between Weston Cliff and Branscombe Mouth.

NTG – From Branscombe Mouth to Beer Head the map does not show the path along the top of Hooken Cliffs only through Under Hooken. It is mentioned in the text. Both routes are official.

NTG – Between Coxe's Cliff and Branscombe the old route is described. Map is also wrong.

BMG – The old route is shown east of Littlecombe Shoot.

70 | Seaton to Lyme Regis

Grading: Moderate	Distance –	12	868	8	542

You leave Seaton across its concrete bridge over the River Axe and have to turn inland. Then, go up the road to the golf course and make a considerable detour to get back onto the coastal path. There have been moves afoot to get the path truly coastal but as yet we have not been successful. If you agree that you would like a coastal path you could drop a line to Devon County Council, or the Countryside Commission, saying just that. It could help.

The section through the Landslip is in a National Nature Reserve and can be very rewarding to some but extremely frustrating to others. Views are extremely limited and the path in places puts on a fair imitation of a corkscrew or helter-skelter; you are unlikely to get lost but most unlikely to know where you are. Suggested times to walk the Landslip range from 1 1/2 hours to 4 hours, but we are told that the standard time is about 3 hours.

The path into Lyme Regis has now been improved and you can take a path directly down to The Cobb without having to come into the car park and then down the road.

(It is easy to miss the start of the path from Lyme. Follow the seafront past the landward end of the Cobb breakwater but turn sharp right as soon as you have passed the bowling green.)

BMG – Page 70. The path does not enter a car park above Lyme Regis. It is through fields direct to The Cobb.

| 71 | Lyme Regis to Charmouth | OS 193 (T) Lyme Regis E/C Th. |

| Grading: Moderate | Distance – | 4 | 872 | 2 | 544 |

Beware the official H.M.S.O. Guide to the Dorset Path which incorrectly describes the way out of Lyme Regis.

This is a difficult section owing to the very insecure nature of the cliffs. Dorset County Council have worked to provide a series of routes here but they are up against a continual problem of slipping cliffs. There have had to be necessary diversions. The last incidence of erosion has prompted the Golf Club to ban all coast path walkers from the edge of their course. This has resulted in Dorset County Council diverting the path to well inland around most of the golf course, and here we are, seven years later, still awaiting Coast Path reinstatement. We think we ought to tell you that having entered Dorset now, that it is quite the worst county on the path at maintenance. Furthermore, it is also the slowest at making good any gaps caused by landslides and also that it has a piece of so-called Coastal Path furthest away from the coast. Having said all that, it does have many sections of extremely good walking if only the county would establish a true coast path which is, after all, what it is supposed to be.

At the time of going to print we have been advised that agreement is close between the golf club and Dorset County Council over a strip of land for a new Coast Path. However for this edition we still include details of the official diversion with our own modifications. If you are lucky enough to find the new path in place 'on the ground' when you come to this section it should be signposted. In any case it is not difficult to follow as it is routed between the golf course and the cliff edge.

From Lyme Regis town centre take Charmouth Road until you reach Spittles Lane. On the right you will find a footpath across fields to a lane where you turn left then shortly turn right to walk the road past the Golf Club House and rejoin the main A3052 road. In a hundred yards or so take the footpath on the right running east. You will drop down across fairways into woodland and following the path which curves to the north you will regain the main A3052 road again. On the way down the hill, near the junction of this road and the new A35 Charmouth Bypass, watch out for a stile and a public footpath on your right. This will take you through Lily Farm and across a field where you come to a road. Turn right. Then within 50 yards, turn left and carry straight on to the coast. (For those travelling east to west: leave Charmouth Beach and follow the coast path. When you arrive at a road, cross it, then at the next – turn right and very shortly on your left you will find a public footpath across a field and going through Lily Farm. This path will bring you out on to the busy A35. Here turn left and 'keeping to the A35' walk uphill and take off on the A3052. As soon as you reach woodlands look out for your footpath on the left. This will take you through those woods and across fairways to the A3052 which is now running south into Lyme Regis. A minor road on the left takes you past the Golf Club House on the left then it's all downhill into Lyme Regis.)

We recommend a low tide diversion along the beach between Lyme Regis and Charmouth especially if the tide is well out because the sand is very firm here. On no account should attempts be made to walk upon the surface of the huge grey mud slide. When the tide permits, keep to seaward on firm sand. If the tide is not sufficiently far out to walk past the river mouth at Lyme, one can take the track down to the beach just beyond the Theatre. (Westward walkers take extreme care before setting off on the beach at Charmouth because the Lyme Regis end gets submerged first by the incoming tide.)

CP – See paragraph above for route through Lily Farm. It is not as that shown on map.

NTG – There is no route alongside the golf course on Timber Hill as shown on the map, although it is referred to in the text. We think this important because many walkers try to work from maps first. This map does show you our recommended track through Lily Farm rather than Dorset County Council's advised route along the main road.

72 | Charmouth to West Bay

OS 193 1 mile to (V) Charmouth E/C Wed.

Grading: Strenuous		Distance –	11	883	7	551

Interesting walking with spectacular views from Cain's Folly and Golden Cap, the highest mainland point on the south coast of England. However, be warned, your good views are not obtained without effort!

When you get to what looks like the top of Golden Cap you have to turn left and go a little higher to the trig. point to find your way down, which starts at the North end before later swinging East again.

73 | West Bay to Abbotsbury (Swannery Car Park)

OS 194

Grading: Moderate		Distance –	15	898	9	560

SEE SECTION 79 FOR DETAILS OF THE ALTERNATIVE INLAND COAST PATH FROM WEST BEXINGTON TO OSMINGTON MILLS.

Leaving West Bay do not go seaward again immediately after you have walked round the back of the harbour. Continue along an un-named street which has St John's Church on the left-hand side as you enter it. Shortly, the main road bends left but still continue forward. The sign for the coast path is opposite The West Bay Hotel pointing at an angle across a gravel yard to the foot of surprisingly steep cliffs. If you go seaward in West Bay too soon you will give yourself a hard stretch along coarse shingle.

Watch for the inland diversion at Burton Freshwater. When the river is low you can 'cut the corner' across the beach but this is not at all possible when the river is flowing strongly; do not try it, you will surely drown! As you start to descend to the caravan park you can look across and see if the river is not reaching the sea, then it is up to you.

At Burton Bradstock Beach just after the hotel the old seasonal cafe that burnt down has been rebuilt by the National Trust, and is leased out by them.

At Burton Mere, unless you are particularly interested in maritime flowers, it is nearly always better to go inland of the Mere, rather than go along the seaward side. You will get quite enough pebbles later.

There is a seasonal cafe at West Bexington, and seasonal snack wagons in the car park where the road turns inland past Abbotsbury Gardens. Walkers, however, should continue along for another couple of hundred yards.

Refreshments, shops and B & B's in Abbotsbury. If you have time the climb up to St Catherine's Chapel is worth the effort.

74 | Abbotsbury (Swannery Car Park) to Weymouth

OS 194

Grading: Easy Chesil Beach: Strenuous		Distance –	23	921	14	574

Presumably you must have wanted to go into Abbotsbury if you did visit the village, but it is worth mentioning that the path does not really go there at all, but only close to it. Therefore, the correct, and sometimes quieter, way out is by the footpath going south to Nunnery Grove, and not the road by Mill Farm.

The path unfortunately now goes over a mile inland, despite our efforts. The inland path is well marked and enjoyable to walk, part of it along a ridge and with some good views. You do not get back to the shores of the Fleet until the stream south of Bridge Lane.

The section until the path gets back to the shores of the Fleet at Rodden Hive, is poorly sign-posted, and the route on the ground does not agree with the map. We have reported all these deficiencies to Dorset County Council; do please let them, and us, know if you still get problems.

A few practical suggestions:-

(a) After Horsepool Farm keep going up the ridge, beguiling, much better tracks go round the hill to the right, but they will not bring you to the stile you need at the top.

(b) Turn sharp left after Hodder's Coppice. The best track goes forward, but this is NOT the one you want.

(c) After you have crossed the minor road, the official path follows the field headland east and then south to the north east corner of Wyke Woods as signposted, and not in a direct line as shown on some maps.

(d) The path just East of Bridge Lane is further away from it on the ground than shown on the map.

(e) Take particular care as you approach Rodden Hive – the path suddenly dives through a hedge on your left. There is an apparent track and even a marker post which might make you think that the path goes to the right of the stream, but it does not.

At Charlestown, one may have to divert if firing on the range is in progress across the definitive right of way. A new diversion has been made inland at Wyke Regis for a Service Establishment.

From Ferrybridge, on last inspection, there were no signs to tell you where to start, where to leave the old railway to get back to the coastal path, or at any junctions to encourage you! We have asked for all of this. However, having some experience of Dorset County Council's tortoise-like speed, we will say you had better watch it, if you are to get the best out of this section. There is a little summer ferry which shortens the route across the harbour at Weymouth.

An alternative for the tough walker who wishes to stay on the coast is to use the Chesil Beach; this is, of course, much more attractive since the inland route has been worsened. You can do this by going onto the beach where the path turns inland at Abbotsbury but note you cannot 'get off' again until you reach the causeway from Wyke Regis to Portland. This is only a walk for the fit and not one to be attempted at times of severe gale! Please note that the Chesil Bank is closed to visitors from 1st May-31st August for the Schedule 1 bird nesting season. During the nesting season please keep to the seaward side of the beach so as not to interfere with nesting birds.

(Going west turn left on the main Portland/Wyke Regis/Weymouth road, turn right across the beach as soon as you can to pick up the Chesil Bank. However, the warnings shown above still apply.)

Weymouth Harbour
Weymouth & Portland Borough Council,
Harbour Master's Office,
Municipal Offices, PO Box 21,
North Quay, Weymouth, DT4 8TA
(0305-206278) Ask for Dep. Borough Engineer.

Seasonal. Easter–October Daily.
Continuous if passengers are waiting
and weather permits.

NTG – The definitive path is now around the edge of Langton Hive Point. It no longer makes the loop inland as shown. North of Wykes Woods the path is as described in (c) above.

| 75 | **Weymouth to West Lulworth** | OS 194 (T) Weymouth E/C Wed. (B. Rail) |

Grading: This section runs the gamut from easy to moderate to strenuous

| | Distance – | 19 | 940 | 12 | 586 |

SEE SECTION 79 FOR DETAILS OF THE ALTERNATIVE INLAND COAST PATH FROM WEST BEXINGTON TO OSMINGTON MILLS.

The start along the seafront at Weymouth has been called uninteresting but at least you are in sight of the sea all the way. When the promenade comes to an end opt for walking along the wall behind the beach; this keeps you away from the traffic and gives you the best view, as long as you do not fall off! At Overcombe where the path leaves the road there is no proper route signposted at the time of writing; the official route should go up the minor road to Bowleaze Cove. However, after passing the Spyglass Inn it is best to cross the grass public open space and follow the cliff edge to the Beachside Centre. After Pontin's Riviera Holiday Centre the cliff is sliding away and the path with it. However, a slight diversion on stable ground is possible.

At the stile at the eastern end of the Pontin's Holiday Camp, this is the second Pontin's establishment and is shown as Short Lake House on maps, a so called temporary diversion starts because the path has been lost in a landslide at Osmington Mills. At the time of going to print a Public path order has been made for a new section of path to avoid the landslip. Hopefully the new route will be in place by the time you walk this section. However details of the diversion, the original route and the new route are given for this year's edition.

The diversion notice contains a map showing the diversion which the Association believes is unsatisfactory and is pressing Dorset C.C. to reinstate the original path or create a suitable alternative close to the coast. However, for the present time the diversion should be followed and its route is marked by rather small indistinct wooden signs displaying a waymark containing a 'D'. If the tide is out – use the beach. The route takes the private access road from the holiday camp to the main A353 road in Osmington Village. Take care as this narrow road is used by coaches and lorries servicing the holiday camp. At the main road it is necessary to cross it and turn right as the only footpath on this busy and dangerous road is on the north side. Continue for some 400 metres through the village and just beyond the speed limit sign re-cross the road at Craigs Farm. The diverted route then follows the Alternative Inland Path described in the penultimate paragraph of Section 79.

(West bound walkers should leave the coast and walk north up the road from Osmington Mills and follow the diverted and Alternative Inland Path to Osmington village. Using the footpath on the north side of the A353 road proceed westwards through the village and cross back to turn south into the access road to the holiday camp (marked with a blue sign indicating 'Pontins'). Just before the perimeter gates to the Camp a stile gives access the field which is crossed in a southerly direction to re-join the Coast Path.)

If the diversion has been removed and you are able to use the true coast path it is important that at the stile at the eastern end of the Holiday Camp that you follow the sign. It does in fact point in the right direction; compass carriers check it – it's about 72°. You go up over the hill apparently going inland – you do not follow the cliff edge. While the Association does not support action that circumvents official diversions it should be mentioned that a faint but rough path has become established through the landslip area. This route is are capable of being used by any reasonable agile walker particularly in dry weather but anybody using it must be aware of the risks or of any further landslips which could occur.

On the downhill approach to Osmington Mills the new route bears away from the cliff edge over a stile and down the right hand side of a field. At the bottom it joins the Alternative Inland Route just before it crosses two stiles to meet the narrow road that is followed down to the coast. The new route should be signposted.

At Ringstead one is taken inland, although the official path should go along the seafront. At the old coastguard cottages at White Nothe, be careful to take the left fork of the two yellow arrows, that being the correct route. From White Nothe onwards you will find that there are some quite severe gradients to be traversed before you reach Lulworth.

There is an unfortunate diversion slightly inland on the last stretch down to Lulworth Cove, however, some people turn even further inland than they need. Some new signposts have been erected in the Lulworth Cove area indicating 'Youth Hostel–Coast Path' and contain the acorn emblem. These signs are intended to indicate the route to the Youth Hostel at East Lulworth and are not the continuation of the Coast Path.

The nimble who wish to arrive at Lulworth by a quieter, non-car-park route, should, on Hambury Tout, turn right and take the old track down on the right-hand side of the fence. This links with the beach path to St Oswald's Bay. On reaching this turn left. Presently, it comes to a tarmac road which you can follow into Lulworth.

NTG – The route shown in the map from Hambury Tout to West Lulworth is the alternative and not the true Coast Path which keeps to seaward and is much more pleasant than walking through a huge car park.

Grading: Severe   Distance –   11   951   7   593

The coastal path through the Army Ranges is now open again at certain times, see below. It is a very fine walk indeed but a tough one. If closed, we now include the walk around, see below.

At most states of the tide, it is perfectly possible to walk along the pebble beach at Lulworth Cove, going up the path which rises diagonally on the far side of the beach. At the top of the steep ascent off the beach, the best route proceeds seawards and there the path turns eastwards along the coast to the beginning of the Army Ranges, just by the Fossil Forest.

If, unfortunately, time should be of the essence, when you have crossed the beach and gone up the path, do not turn right but go straight ahead. This way you will come to the Bindon Gate into the range, and you can go ahead here coming out on the coast again at Mupe Bay. It is a little shorter but far less scenic.

RAC Gunnery School Lulworth Ranges: No Firing and Firing Periods

1. *NON FIRING PERIOD.* The Range Walks will be open to the public during the following holiday periods: All dates are inclusive:

   a. CHRISTMAS/NEW YEAR 1992/93   18 DEC 92–04 JAN 93
   b. EASTER 1993   09 APR 93–18 APR 93
   c. SPRING 1993   29 MAY 93–06 JUN 93
   d. SUMMER 1993   31 JUL 93–05 SEP 93
   e. CHRISTMAS 1993/94   18 DEC 93–02 JAN 94

2. *Firing Periods.* The Range Walks are normally open to the public every Saturday and Sunday except for some weekends in the year. For 1993 they have reserved the following 6 weekends for firing:

   a. FIRST WEEKEND   30–31 JAN 93
   b. SECOND WEEKEND   27–28 MAR 93
   c. THIRD WEEKEND   08–09 MAY 93
   d. FOURTH WEEKEND   03–04 JUL 93
   e. FIFTH WEEKEND   09–10 OCT 93
   f. SIXTH WEEKEND   27–28 NOV 93

3. Experience has shown that it is sometimes possible to avoid firing on some of these reserved weekends and if this is the case the Range Walks will be opened. Should this occur in 1993 they will make every effort to publicise the fact.

4. Tyneham Church and the School are normally open for viewing 0900 hrs–1500 hrs when the Walks are open.

5. Information is also available from:

a. The Range Control Office. (0900-1630 hours Mon-Fri and during the six weekend firing periods). Telephone Bindon Abbey (0929) 462721 Ext 4819/4859.

b. The Guardroom (at any time). Telephone: Bindon Abbey (0929) 462721 Ext 4824.

Unfortunately, there are no permanent staff on duty in the Guardroom. Soldiers posted to or on a course at Lulworth find themselves on Guard Duty from time to time. They have much to do and whether or not the Range Walks are open does not come at the top of the list. Every effort is made to ensure that up to date information is to hand at the Guardroom.

If the ranges are shut there is no option but to follow the B3070 north east for 5 miles to GR 886855 at West Holme. Turn right (signposted Stoborough) and a further 1½ miles along the road turn right just before a hump-back railway bridge on to Dorey Farm bridleway at GR 912855. After

1¼ miles turn right on to Creech Road leading south-southwest towards the Purbeck Ridge. Another 1½ miles road walk up a steep gradient to a viewpoint car park. Beyond the car park (902815) take the left road that turns back and down over the ridge to Corfe. (A short cut bridleway at 905817 zig-zags down to meet the same road). As the road levels out at a left hand bend (907812) take the bridleway ahead that leads out south through Steeple Leaze Farm. 200 yards south of the farm a footpath leads south crossing another ridge bridleway, down a steep path, and across a field to Higher Stonehips, and on to Gaulter Gap, the easterly point of the range walks (11 miles).

This Association has commenced enquiries in an effort to obtain a more pleasant, and shorter route using footpaths and bridleways.

---

77 | Kimmeridge, Gaulter Gap to Swanage

OS 195

Grading: Severe and then moderate	Distance –	19	970	12	605

From Gaulter Gap, Kimmeridge, there is a good path all the way to Chapman's Pool. We used to mention an alternative, of walking along the Kimmeridge Ledges using some steps at Encombe. However, the steps periodically disappear and return. (The only recommended use can now be east to west if at Encombe and it is low tide and there are steps, you can go to Kimmeridge along the beach and ledges. It makes for a different sort of walking but do not expect to save time, and as always, watch the tide.)

There had been problems between Chapman's Pool and St Albans Head in the undercliff area. Unfortunately, we have had to agree to a new high level route, and this has increased the distance by about one mile. The path is very well signposted in general. There is one place, after you have turned inland where you reach a gate in a field by a cattle grid, where you could go wrong. You must not go over the cattle grid where the signpost says, 'The Beach is Closed' but instead follow the path which bears inland up the valley and when the houses are reached there are plenty of signs to guide you from there on.

The first part of the climb up West Hill is uninteresting and sadly away from shoulder and views. However as you gain height going along Emmets Hill views back along the Dorset Coast are very good indeed. Do not miss the new Royal Marines memorial just to the left of the path and be sure to read the inscription.

From St Albans Head there is fine high level walking all the way to Durleston Head. There is not much accommodation along this stretch. There is a poor bus service from Worth Matravers to Swanage, so plan ahead.

There is a total absence of signing in the Durleston Head Countryside Park. Again we have asked for improvement so it may be there when you get there. However, you keep on the low level path all the way around Durleston Head but as you come up on the north side of it you take the second turning right not the first which is a dead end into a quarry.

The section of the coastal path is not very clear in and around Swanage, but you are unlikely to get badly lost. At high tide the Official Path just south east of Swanage can be under water!

CP – The map suggests that the Coast Path enters Worth Matravers. It does not. It turns sharply south through the word 'Farm' of Renscombe Farm.

---

78 | Swanage to Sandbanks (South Haven Point)

OS 195 (T) Swanage E/C Th. (V) Studland E/C Th.

Grading: Moderate	Distance –	12	982	8	613

At Ocean Bay Stores at the north end of Swanage Sea Front, tide permitting, it is usually better to keep along the pedestrian promenade to the end and then walk 200 yards along the beach turning up some steps rather than take the poor Official. If it is high tide and you have to follow the latter route leave the seafront on the main road (Ulwell Road) and where it bears left into a one-way system continue ahead into Redcliffe Road. At the sub Post Office turn sharp right into Ballard Way and at the end do not be put off by the signs 'Ballard Private Estate'. Carry forward into the quaint little estate of chalets and follow signs for the Coast Path to emerge on to a grassed area on the cliff edge.

Signposting is bad in Studland. As you come in you reach a road junction by a public toilet. Here turn right. You will then pass two Public Footpath signs pointing right, but do not take either of them. Eventually, you will come to The Manor House Hotel. It is the track/road down to the beach after this hotel that you require. When you get down to the beach, turn left. When the tide is out this is firm, but when it is in more effort is required. Maybe too we should warn those who do not know, that this is a naturist beach, so you must not be put off if you find on this last lap that you are the only one wearing clothes!

Wainwright at the end of his work on the Pennine Way said it all, and said it better, of a shorter path. Ward & Mason in the old Letts Guide simply say 'That's it'. We will add whether you have been lucky enough to walk the whole way from Minehead at one go, or simply, as most of us have, in bits and pieces over a period, nonetheless you will be glad you walked and have just finished Britain's longest and finest footpath. It's a longer step than most take in their lifetime!

IF YOU WISH TO WALK ON, THE BOURNEMOUTH COAST PATH LINKS THE END OF THE SOUTH WEST WAY WITH THE RECENTLY WAYMARKED SOLENT WAY, GIVING A CONTINUOUS PATH FROM MINEHEAD TO EMSWORTH.

Studland/Sandbanks (Mouth of Poole Harbour) Bournemouth-Swanage Motor Road & Ferry Company, Shell Bay, Studland. BH19 3BA.
Tel: Studland (0929) 44203.

All year round (except for approx. 2 weeks in Nov). Every 20 minutes, less during peak periods. Late ferry 2300 hrs. At weekends and throughout the summer every night.

79   Alternative Inland Coast Path: West Bexington to Osmington Mills   OS 194

Grading: Moderate   Distance –   29   18

Although this is certainly not a coastal path it is an enjoyable walk along a well-marked path with good views seaward from the ridges.

At West Bexington car park turn inland up the road signposted 'Inland Route – Coast Path', and where the road turns left, continue forward up a stony track, signposted 'Hardy Monument 5½ miles' and at next junction turn right, signposted 'Hardy Monument 5 miles'. At top of the hill the footpath briefly joins the main road but you immediately leave again over the stile through the field, signposted 'Hardy Monument 5 miles'. Take care, the way across this field is not clear and one must keep to the bottom end of the field and not stay along the top wire fence. After you have crossed the wall, you can start to bear upwards to the left to the further signpost near the road, marked with the acorn symbol and the words 'Inland Route'. After about 300 yards continuing through the field and by the corner of a wall there is a further signpost 'Hardy Monument 4½, Osmington Mills 15'. Continue forward, very shortly emerging on to the B3157 road which you cross and leave through a gate, signposted 'Hardy Monument 4½'. The footpath through the field which you have just crossed is very indistinct. However, this does not matter too much as long as you eventually emerge on the road at this point.

You now approach Abbotsbury Castle and where the path in front divides take the right-hand fork along the front of the Fort past the trig point, from where you can get superb views in both directions, and then proceed forward to the road. From the trig point you should be able to see clearly Hardy's Monument in the distance showing you the way forward. Cross the minor road now and go forward, signpost 'Hardy Monument 4'. Proceed forward along the ridge through a gate and across a field to a stile with an acorn mark, shortly reaching a three-direction signpost indicating the way forward, 'Hardy Monument 3 miles'. Be careful here, the signpost down the valley, 'Abbotsbury ¾ mile' also shows an acorn in error, and you will come across other signposts with the acorn shown wrongly although now fading. Next fence signpost says 'Inland Route – Hardy Monument' with no acorn symbol. There are in fact three gates here but proceed into the field over the stile, waymarked and with an acorn sign.

Continue through the next gate, signposted 'Hardy Monument', and as you cross the next field, the village of Abbotsbury lies below in the valley, with the old chapel clearly visible. At the far side of the field bear left as signposted and leave in the inland corner through a gate on to a minor road. Turn left along the road for approximately 30 yards and then turn right, signposted 'Inland Route – Hardy Monument 2'. Follow the bridle way marked with blue arrows along the wire fence above the scrub to a stile where the blue bridle arrow points to the right and the yellow footpath arrow with acorn indicates the way forward. At the far side of the field the track then leads approximately 50 yards to a further gate with stile and waymark. Immediately adjacent to this gate is a stone circle which is an ancient monument and there is a suitable sign to this effect. One now continues forward, leaving a small wood to the left, to reach the road from Portisham to Winterbourne Steepleton. Turn left along the road for approximately 40 yards and then turn right into a field over a stile, signposted 'Hardy Monument 1½ – Osmington Mills 13'. On the far side of the field proceed forward, signpost 'Hardy Monument 1'. At this point there is a signpost forking right to Hellstone only with a return possible on a different path.

At Blackdown Barn turn left to climb up through the woods, signpost 'Hardy Monument ½'. At the monument you will find a small signpost 'Inland Route – Osmington Mills 11 miles' with a blue arrow indicating the way forward. Cross the road to a further signpost with acorn symbol and now descend through the bracken. One shortly reaches the road again, turn left and in a few yards ignore the signpost on the right, cutting back indicating 'Bridleway to Coast Path' and continue forward, signpost 'Coast Path East' and in another 50 yards turn right, signpost 'Inland Route to Courton Hill' on one side of the sign and 'Osmington 12 – Courton Hill 2' on the other. Now there is a good ridgeway path without navigational problems and good views to the seaward in the distance. Next sign 'Inland Route East' and when you come to three parallel pylon lines you go forward passing under all three. By the first of these electric cables there is a gateway on the right with blue Bridleway arrows indicting a right turn but ignore these and proceed forward. At another gate on your right marked with blue and yellow arrows continue straight forward. After passing the radio mast you come to the B3159 marked by the Borough of Weymouth boundary stone, continue across the road, signposted 'Inland Route East'.

On reaching the A354 turn right immediately before the main road down the signposted track and after just over ¼ mile you will find a stile in the hedge on your left. The path leads across a narrow field to cross the busy A354. Before the farm with its adjacent radio mast take care to go through the gate on the right, marked with a blue arrow, but this time also with the acorn symbol. After crossing the field, leaving two tumuli to your left, you reach a metalled road. Turn right and at the next junction there is a signpost surmounted by a symbol 'Dorset – Came Wood' which, unusually, carries the six-figure map reference of the locality. Here you turn right at the signpost 'Bridleway to Bincombe' and the acorn symbol. At the end of the path join a metalled road and at the junction turn left, signposted 'Inland Route East'.

Drop down the road into the village of Bincombe and where the road turns right take the track up leaving a small church on your right. Where the path splits take the left-hand fork signposted again with a blue arrow and the acorn symbol. After the overhead high-voltage power lines pass through a small signposted wooden gate and then proceed forward through one field into the next to the footpath sign. Here turn half left, following the line of the old indistinct curving grassy track until it meets the road at the bottom of Combe Valley. Turn left here and follow the road until you reach the Combe Valley road sign to 'Sutton Poyntz' and take this turn to the right. After 50 yards turn left through a gate, signposted 'White Horse Hill – Osmington Mills'. The path now is easy to follow with extensive views to seaward over Weymouth and Portland. On passing a ruined building on your left you reach a broad track and turn right, signposted 'Osmington 1½' and after about 300 yards leave the track through a gate on the right, signposted 'Inland Route Osmington'. You will shortly pass the trig point on your right and at the next field gate turn left and follow the field boundary along White Horse Hill. Just beyond the next gate fork right, signpost 'Osmington 1, Lulworth 8'.

Descend to the village of Osmington and follow the signs through the village to Osmington Mills. When you reach the main Weymouth road at the Sun Ray Inn turn left and in about 200 yards turn right over a stile into a field, crossing diagonally in the direction of the arrow. Cross the next field diagonally and at the top look back to see Hardy's Monument in the distance and also the white horse on the hillside. Go over the stile to the footpath sign, turn half right to cross the field at an angle to a further stile. Cross it and turn left along the hedge side to the bottom. At the end of the field there is a very short length of enclosed footpath to the road, turn right along it descending to Osmington Mills.

When walking this section bear in mind that we found no place for obtaining refreshments between the start of the walk, where there is a cafe, and the village of Osmington.

ACCOMMODATION

This list of accommodation has been prepared in path order anti-clockwise.

Regarding the left-hand column P = Packed lunches available.

O = Open all the year.
D = Drying facilities for wet clothes.

The part of the address in CAPITALS is an aid to location. It does not signify the postal town.

The extreme right hand column refers to the appropriate section in the "Trail Description" part. We think it might help walkers find addresses quickly.

The amount in brackets after the address gives an indication of the starting price for bed and breakfast. If working on a tight budget it is best to ask first.

Telephone numbers are now shown with the exchange first, STD code second and number last.
In respect of the hostels listed, greater details will be found in the Hostel Handbook, available from Youth Hostels Association (England & Wales), St Albans, Herts. AL1 2DY. In particular watch the closed periods of the hostels.

We wish to develop this list especially for many 'sparse' areas. Suggestions for inclusion in our next list will be welcome. Details of any new accommodation should be addressed to the Membership Secretary.

Our list is not comprehensive, walkers will find many B&B's in towns and villages along the coast path that are not recorded in this book.

It would not be out of place here to add a word of thanks from those who walk to those who kindly board. How many times have we been thankful for a friendly welcome and good 'digs'? Maybe a note we had from one of our accommodation addresses puts it well. "We have had quite a lot of walkers this year and we have usually managed to dry them out – and feed them up."

Although there are a lot of addresses that state they are 'open all the year', some of these close for the Christmas period.

Walkers should remember that during the holiday season many of our accommodation addresses could be fully booked up in advance by holidaymakers staying for a week or two. Conversely a walker could book up for one night only in good time thus preventing a guest house proprietor from taking a week or more booking later on. Accommodation problems can be frustrating to all parties concerned so bear these facts in mind when bed hunting.

During your initial contact with your selected host you could ask – 'Do you pick up and return to the coast path?' 'Do you provide early breakfasts?'And, if it should bother you that much, 'are there smokers in the house?'

Important If having booked ahead, and for some reason or other you do not arrive at your accommodation address please telephone and explain your absence to your intended host. We have known instances where the host has become so worried about the non-appearance of walkers that they have informed the emergency services. The last thing we want is Police, Coastguards and Royal Navy helicopters out on a wild goose chase.

If you are making an extended walk over some weeks you might like to consider the advantage of opening an account with Girobank. You will find many more post offices than you will banks furthermore the post offices are open for longer hours. We have met folk who lost a whole day's walking waiting for the right day for their own bank to be open!

TOURIST INFORMATION CENTRES can be a source of B & B addresses. If you have difficulties in booking accommodation then they should be approached. To help we have included details of TIC's in the appropriate path order in this accommodation section.

P	O	D	Name and Address	Telephone No.	Map Ref.	Section

SOMERSET

YOUTH HOSTEL MINEHEAD – SEE Y.H.A. SECTION PAGE

P	O	D	Name and Address	Telephone No.	Map Ref.	Section
			Tourist Information Centre, 17 Friday Street, MINEHEAD, Somerset.	0643 702624		1
*	*	*	Mrs D Morris, Badgers, 38 Summerland Road, MINEHEAD, Somerset. (£12.00)	0643 704583		1
*	*	*	Mr M Morris, The Parks Hotel, The Parks, MINEHEAD, Somerset, TA24 8BT. (£15.00)	0643 703547	965 463	1
*		*	Mr & Mrs J & A Segenhout, Mayfair Hotel, The Avenue, MINEHEAD, Somerset, TA24 5AY. (£22.00)	0643 702719		1
*	*	*	Mrs S Coombes, Hurlstone, Sparkhayes Lane, PORLOCK, Somerset. (£13.00)	0643 862650	887 469	1
*	*	*	Mr E Bower, Countrywide Holidays, Doverhay Place, PORLOCK, Somerset, TA24 8EX. (£15.00)	0643 862398	891 468	1
*	*	*	Mr & Mrs M & J Robinson, The Ship Inn, PORLOCK, Somerset, TA24 8QD. (£16.50)	0643 862507		1
*	*	*	Mrs J Stiles-Cox, Leys, The Ridge, Off Bossington Lane, PORLOCK, Somerset, TA24 8HA. (£14.00)	0643 862477	892 469	1
	*	*	Mr D Thorne, Myrtle Cottage, High Street, PORLOCK, Somerset TA24 8PU. (£15.00)	0643 862978	885 468	1
*	*	*	Mr & Mrs R G Thornton, Lorna Doone Hotel, High Street, PORLOCK, Somerset, TA24 8PS. (£18.50)	0643 862404	888 468	1
*	*	*	Mrs B Starr, Sea View Cottage, PORLOCK WEIR, Somerset. (£13.50)	0643 862523	864 478	1
*	*	*	Mrs E J Richards, Silcombe Farm, PORLOCK, Somerset. (£14.00)	0643 862248		1

NORTH DEVON

YOUTH HOSTELS LYNTON, ILFRACOMBE – SEE Y.H.A. SECTION PAGE

P	O	D	Name and Address	Telephone No.	Map Ref.	Section
*		*	Mr & Mrs A Hawkins, Tregonwell, 1 Tors Road, LYNMOUTH, Devon, EX35 6ET. (£16.00)	0598 53369	726 494	2
*		*	North Cliff Hotel, North Walk, LYNMOUTH, EX35 6HJ. (£22.50)	0598 52357		2
*	*	*	Mrs J Pile, Oakleigh, 4 Tors Road, LYNMOUTH, EX35 6ET. (£16.00)	0598 52220		2

P	O	D	Name and Address	Telephone No.	Map Ref.	Section
*		*	Mr & Mrs Price, East Lyn House Hotel, Watersmeet Road, LYNMOUTH, EX35 6EP. (£22.00)	0598 52540		2
	*	*	Mrs B Watts, Rocklyn, 27 Tors Road, LYNMOUTH, North Devon. (£15.00)	0598 52233		2
*	*	*	Mrs P E Morgan, Kingford House, Longmead, LYNTON, North Devon. (£17.00)	0598 52361		2
*	*	*	Mr & Mrs J & R Oborne, The Retreat, No 1 Park Gardens, Lydiate Lane, LYNTON, North Devon, EX35 6DF. (£14.00)	0598 53526		2
*	*	*	Woodlands Hotel, Lynbridge, LYNTON, EX35 6AX. (£25.00)	0598 52324	721 493	2
			Tourist Information Centre, Town Hall, Lee Road, LYNTON, EX35 6BT.	0598 52225		2
		*	Mrs Dallyn, Mannacott Farm, MARTINHOE, Devon. (£12.50)	05983 227	663 482	2
*	*	*	Mr & Mrs F J Barry, Glendower, King Street, COMBE MARTIN, Devon, EX34 0AL (£12.00)	0271 883449		3
*		*	Mrs J Bosley, Hillview Guest House, The Woodlands, COMBE MARTIN, North Devon. (£13.00)	0271 882331	575 469	3
*	*	*	Mr & Mrs Clarke, Wynnestead, King Street, COMBE MARTIN, North Devon. (£11.50)	0271 883363		3
*	*	*	Mr R Leonard, The Fo'c's'le, Seaside, COMBE MARTIN, Devon, EX34 0DJ. (£19.50)	0271 883354		3
*	*	*	Saffron House Hotel, King Street, COMBE MARTIN, EX34 0BX. (£15.00)	0271 883521		3
*		*	Mrs A Waldon, Idlehour, Borough Road, COMBE MARTIN, EX34 0AN. (£11.00)	0271 883217		3
			Tourist Information Centre, Sea Cottage, Cross Street, COMBE MARTIN, EX34 0DH.	0271 883319		3
*	*	*	Mr & Mrs A G Furber, Slipway Cottage, 2 Hierns Lane, The Harbour, ILFRACOMBE, EX34 9EH. (£14.00)	0271 863035		4
*		*	Mrs M Howard, 2 Capstone Place, ILFRACOMBE, EX34 9TQ. (£12.50)	0271 865201		4
*	*	*	Mr D Jackson, The Royal Britannia Hotel, The Harbour, ILFRACOMBE, Devon. (£16.00)	0271 862939		4
*	*	*	Mr & Mrs Winearls, Norbury, Torrs Park, ILFRACOMBE, EX34 8AZ. (£13.50)	0271 863888		4
			Tourist Information Centre, The Promenade, ILFRACOMBE, EX34 9BX.	0271 863001		4
*	*	*	Mrs Fran Nustedt, The Grampus Inn, LEE BAY, Near Ilfracombe. (£15.00)	0271 862906		5

P	O	D	Name and Address	Telephone No.	Map Ref.	Section
		*	Mr P Blackmore, Higher Warcombe Cottage, MORTEHOE, EX34 7EJ. (£12.50)	0271 870503	478 458	5
*		*	Lundy House Hotel, MORTEHOE. (£17.00)	0271 870372		5
	*	*	Mrs A Braund, Clyst House, Rockfield Road, WOOLACOMBE, EX34 7DH. (£13.00)	0271 870220		6
*	*	*	Mr & Mrs S Bryant, Sunnyside Hotel, Sunnyside Road, WOOLACOMBE, EX34 7DG. (£14.00)	0271 870267		6
*	*	*	Mrs T Gyles, Ocean View, The Esplanade, WOOLACOMBE, EX34 7DJ. (£12.50)	0271 870359		6
*	*	*	Mr & Mrs H Riley, Camberley, Beach Road, WOOLACOMBE. (£16.00)	0271 870231	437 464	6
			Tourist Information Centre, Hall 70, Beach Road, WOOLACOMBE, EX34 7BT.	0271 870553		6
*		*	Mr & Mrs C & R Gedling, West Winds Guest House, Moor Lane, CROYDE, EX33 1PA. (£19.00)	0271 890489		7
*		*	Mrs J Windsor, Chapel Farm, Hobbs Hill, CROYDE. (£16.00)	0271 890429	444 391	7
*	*	*	Mrs E Dale, 2 Linksview, SAUNTON, Braunton. (£12.00)	0271 812233		8
*	*	*	Mr & Mrs M & W Sargent, Alexander Brookdale Hotel, 62 South Street, BRAUNTON, EX33 2AN. (£16.50)	0271 812075		8
*	*	*	Mrs R C Saunders, Stockwell Lodge, 66 South Street, BRAUNTON. (£15.00)	0271 814338	486 361	8
*	*	*	Mrs Jean Watkins, North Cottage, 14 North Street, BRAUNTON, EX33 1AJ. (£12.50)	0271 812703	485 367	8
			Tourist Information Centre, Caen Street Car Park, BRAUNTON, EX33 1AA.	0271 816400		8
*	*	*	Mr & Mrs B & O Capp, Crossways, Braunton Road, BARNSTAPLE, EX31 1JY. (£13.50)	0271 79120	555 333	8
*	*	*	Newholme Guest House, Bickington Road, Sticklepath, BARNSTAPLE. EX31 2DB. (£12.00)	0271 72715		8
	*	*	Miss L M Tucker, Enfield, Top of Sticklepath Hill, BARNSTAPLE, EX31 2DW. (£15.00)	0271 22949		8
			Tourist Information Centre, North Devon Library, Tuly Street, BARNSTAPLE, EX31 1TY.	0271 47177		8

P	O	D	Name and Address	Telephone No.	Map Ref.	Section
*	*	*	Mrs D E George, Oakwood, 34 Yelland Road, Fremington, BARNSTAPLE, EX31 3DS. (£10.50)	0271 73884		9
*	*	*	Mount Hotel, Northdown Road, BIDEFORD, EX39 3LP. (£16.00)	0237 473748	449 269	9
			Tourist Information Centre, Victoria Park, The Quay, BIDEFORD, EX39 2QQ.	0237 477676		9
*	*	*	Mrs M Cox, Riverside Guest House, 4 Marine Parade, APPLEDORE, EX39 1PJ. (£12.00)	0237 478649		9
*	*	*	Mr M Cove, The Royal Hotel, Market Street, APPLEDORE, EX39 1PS. (£16.00)	0237 474305		9
*	*	*	Mr & Mrs M Federl, Locksley House, 1 Tower Street, NORTHAM, EX39 1JL. (£11.00)	0237 474885		9
*	*	*	Mrs Clegg, Mayfield, Avon Lane, WESTWARD HO! (£12.00)	0237 477128		9
*	*	*	Mrs G P Ross, Beachside, Golf Links Road, WESTWARD HO!, EX39 1LH (£12.50)	0237 477021		9
*	*	*	Mr M Walker, Eversley, 1 Youngaton Road, WESTWARD HO! (£13.50)	0237 471603		9
*	*	*	Mrs J Gould, The Old Mill, BUCKS MILL, Devon. (£12.50)	0237 431701		10
*	*	*	Mrs Curtis, Fuchsia Cottage, Burscott Lane, HIGHER CLOVELLY. (£11.00)	0237 431398	313 241	10
*	*	*	Mrs A Jewell, Burscott Farm, HIGHER CLOVELLY, EX39 5RR. (£12.50)	02374 31252	313 241	10
*	*	*	Mrs J Johns, Dyke Green Farm, HIGHER CLOVELLY, EX39 5RU. (£14.00)	0237 431279/699	311 237	10
*	*	*	Mrs P Vanstone, The Old Smithy, Slerra, HIGHER CLOVELLY, EX39 5ST. (£13.50)	0237 431202		10
*	*	*	Mrs Y Heard, West Titchberry, HARTLAND POINT, EX39 6AU. (£12.50)	0237 441287	242 272	11
*	*	*	Mrs H Davey, Stoke Barton Farm, Stoke, HARTLAND, EX39 0DU. (£15.00)	0237 441238	234 246	11
		*	Mrs G Heard, Ekiya, 15 Brimacombe Road, HARTLAND, North Devon. (£11.00)	0237 441539		11
*	*	*	Mrs B Slee, Homeleigh, Stoke, HARTLAND, EX39 6DU (on coast path). (£14.00)	0237 441465		11
*		*	Mr & Mrs Johns, Hartland Quay Hotel, HARTLAND, EX39 6DU. (£18.50)	0237 441371/281		11

P	O	D	Name and Address	Telephone No.	Map Ref.	Section
*	*	*	Mrs B Downs, Strawberry Water, WELCOMBE MOUTH, EX39 6HL. (£13.50)	028883 403		12
*	*	*	Old Smithy Inn, WELCOMBE, EX39 6HG. (£16.00)	028883 305	227 184	12

NORTH CORNWALL

P	O	D	Name and Address	Telephone No.	Map Ref.	Section
*	*	*	Mrs D Cholwill, Darzle Farm, Woodford, MORWENSTOW, Bude, Cornwall. (£15.00)	028883 222	221 140	12
*	*	*	Mrs I Heard, Dene Farm, MORWENSTOW, Bude, EX23 9SL. (£15.00)	028883 330	226 145	12
*	*	*	Mrs M C Heywood, Cornakey Farm, MORWENSTOW, EX23 9SS. (£14.00)	0288 331260		12
*	*	*	Mrs S A Trevin, Lower Northcott Farm, POUGHILL, Bude, Cornwall. (£15.00)	0288 352350		12
*	*	*	Brendon Arms, BUDE, Cornwall. (£15.00)	0288 354542		12
*	*	*	E & L Hatch, Seaview, 51 Killerton Road, BUDE, EX23 8EN. (£17.00)	0288 352665		12
*		*	Mrs G Hill, Corisande Hotel, 24 Downs View, BUDE, EX23 8RG. (£14.00)	0288 353474		12
*	*	*	Mr & Mrs P Kimpton, Kisauni, 4 Downs View, BUDE. (£11.00)	0288 352653		12
*		*	Mornish Hotel, Summerleaze Crescent, BUDE, EX23 8HJ. (£18.50)	0288 352972	221 140	12
*	*	*	Mr M E Payne, Pencarrol Guest House, 21 Downs View, BUDE, EX23 8RF. (£13.50)	0288 352478		12
*		*	The Meva-Gwin Hotel, Upton, BUDE, EX23 0LY. (£18.00)	0288 352347		12
*		*	Mrs Warburton, Crooklets Inn, Crooklets, BUDE. (£12.50)	0288 352335		12
			Tourist Information Centre, Crescent Car Park, BUDE, EX23 8LE	0288 354240		12
*	*	*	Bay View Inn, WIDEMOUTH BAY, Bude, EX23 0AW. (£12.00)	0288 361273	201 020	13
*		*	Mrs M K Frost, Farthings, Coast Road, WIDEMOUTH BAY, EX23 0LZ. (£11.00)	0288 361348	201 039	13
*	*	*	Mr Marks, Penhalt Farm, WIDEMOUTH BAY. (£12.00)	0288 361210	195 002	13
*		*	Trelawny Hotel, Marine Drive, WIDEMOUTH BAY, EX23 0AH. (£18.00)	0288 361328		13

P	O	D	Name and Address	Telephone No.	Map Ref.	Section
*	*	*	Mr & Mrs J & A Connell, Gunnedah House, CRACKINGTON HAVEN, EX23 0JZ. (£14.00)	0840 230265	140 966	13
*		*	Coombe Barton Inn, CRACKINGTON HAVEN, EX23 0JG. (£14.50)	08403 345		
	*	*	Mrs R Crocker, Tregather, CRACKINGTON HAVEN, EX23 0LQ. (£12.50)	08403 667		13
*	*	*	Mrs E A Redman, 8 Penkenna Close, CRACKINGTON HAVEN, EX23 0PF. (£12.50)	0840 230413	155 956	13

YOUTH HOSTELS BOSCASTLE, TINTAGEL, PADSTOW, NEWQUAY, PERRANPORTH – SEE Y.H.A. SECTION PAGE

P	O	D	Name and Address	Telephone No.	Map Ref.	Section
*	*	*	Mr & Mrs Fillery, Forrabury House, Forrabury Common, BOSCASTLE, PL35 0DJ. (£13.50)	0840 250469		14
*	*	*	Mrs C Nicholls, Trerosewill Farm, Paradise, BOSCASTLE, PL35 0DL. (£15.00)	0840 250545	096 905	14
*		*	Mrs A Jones, Grange Cottage, BOSSINEY, Tintagel, PL34 0AX. (£14.00)	0840 770487	065 887	15
*	*	*	L N Leeds, Willapark Manor Hotel, BOSSINEY, Tintagel, PL34 0BA. (£23.00)	0840 770782		15
*	*	*	Mr & Mrs V Gross, Pendrin House, Atlantic Road, TINTAGEL, PL34 0DE. (£12.50)	0840 770560	056 888	15
*	*	*	Mr T A Read, Trevillett Mill Trout Farm, Rocky Valley, TINTAGEL, PL34 0BB. (£14.00)	0840 770564	075 892	15
*		*	Mr & Mrs D E Wilson, The Riggs, Bossiney Road, TINTAGEL, PL34 0AH. (£12.00)	0840 770427	058 884	15
*	*	*	Mrs K Castle, Dunoon Guest House, 12 Tintagel Terrace, PORT ISAAC, PL29 3SE. (£11.00)	0208 880383	998 810	15
*	*	*	Mrs J Corrigan, The Homestead, Tintagel Terrace, PORT ISAAC, PL29 3SE. (£12.50)	0208 880064		15
*		*	Mrs G Hooper, Gwel Arvor, Tintagel Terrace, PORT ISAAC, PL29 3SE. (£11.50)	0208 880404		15
*	*	*	Old School Hotel Guest House and Restaurant, PORT ISAAC. (£16.50)	0208 880721	996 808	16
*	*	*	St Andrews Hotel, PORT ISAAC, PL29 3SG. (£17.00)	0208 880240	001 809	16
*	*	*	Mr & Mrs R A Mackay, White Lodge Hotel, POLZEATH, PL27 6TJ. (£15.00)	0208 862370		17

P	O	D	Name and Address	Telephone No.	Map Ref.	Section
*	*	*	Mrs M Pashley, Pentire View Guest House, POLZEATH, PL27 6TB. (£12.50)	0208 862484		17
*	*	*	Mr M Martin, Silvermead, ROCK, Wadebridge, PL27 6LB. (£15.00)	020886 2425		18
*		*	Roskarnon House Hotel, ROCK, Wadebridge, PL27 6LD. (£17.50)	0208 862329		18
*	*	*	Mr & Mrs E Champion, 8 Treverbyn Road, PADSTOW, PL28 8DW. (£14.00)	0841 532551		18
		*	Mrs E McGregor, 2 Dennis Road, PADSTOW, PL28 8DD. (£14.25)	0841 532767		18
*	*	*	Mr & Mrs J Stock, Woodlands Close, Tretor, PADSTOW, PL28 8RU. (£14.00)	0841 533109	906 752	18
			Tourist Information Centre, North Quay, PADSTOW, PL28 8AF.	0841 533449		18
*		*	Mrs S Hamilton, Trevone Bay Hotel, TREVONE, Padstow, PL28 8QS. (£18.50)	0841 520243	892 755	19
*	*	*	Treyarnon Bay Hotel, TREYARNON BAY, Padstow, PL28 8DD. (£15.00)	0841 520235	860 740	20
*		*	Mr B Coombes, Bay House Hotel, PORTHCOTHAN BAY, Padstow. (£16.00).	0841 520472		20
*	*	*	Mr & Mrs J M Shadbolt, Trelooan, PORTHCOTHAN, Padstow, PL28 8LS. (£12.00)	0841 521158	858 716	20
*	*	*	Mrs C Lambert, Double K Hotel, Trevarrian, MAWGAN PORTH, TR8 4AQ. (£12.50)	0637 860422		21
*	*	*	Mr & Mrs C Robinson, Sea Vista Hotel, MAWGAN PORTH, TR8 4AL. (£14.00)	0637 860276		21
*	*	*	Tanzarra Villa, Tredragon Road, MAWGAN PORTH, TR7 4DQ. (£12.50)	0637 860628		21
*		*	White Lodge Hotel, MAWGAN PORTH, TR8 4BN. (£17.50)	0637 860512		21
*		*	Mr G Stevenson, Hotel Trevalsa, Watergate Road, Porth, NEWQUAY, TR7 3LX. (£20.00)	0637 873336		21
*	*	*	Mr & Mrs A Hart, Portafino Hotel,, 56 Penhallow Road, Porth, NEWQUAY, TR7 3BY. (£14.00)	0637 875589	829 626	21

P	O	D	Name and Address	Telephone No.	Map Ref.	Section
*	*	*	D & A Connor, Belair Guest House, 28 Edgcumbe Avenue, NEWQUAY, TR7 2NH. (£12.00)	0637 876503		21
*		*	Corisande Manor Hotel, Riverside Ave., Pentire, NEWQUAY, TR7 1PL. (£20.00)	0637 872042		21
*	*	*	Crantock Plains Farmhouse, Cubert, NEWQUAY, TR8 5PH. (£14.00)	0637 830253		21
*		*	S R Harper, Chichester, 14 Bay View, NEWQUAY, TR7 2LR. (£9.00)	0637 874216		21
*	*	*	Mrs M Atkinson, Springvale Guest House, 112 Henver Road, NEWQUAY, TR7 3EQ. (£13.00)	0637 873857	830 620	21
*	*	*	Newlands Guest House, 120 Mount Wise, NEWQUAY, TR7 1QD. (£12.95)	0637 874535		21
*		*	Mrs S Schofield, Hemick Lodge, 33 Pentire Ave., NEWQUAY, TR7 1PB. (£12.50)	0637 872592		21
*	*	*	St Mawes Hotel, Springfield Road, NEWQUAY, TR7 1RT. (£12.00)	0637 872754		21
*	*	*	Tregurrian Hotel, Watergate Bay, NEWQUAY, TR8 4AB. (£17.00)	0637 860280	844 649	21
			Tourist Information Centre, Municipal Offices, Marcus Hill, NEWQUAY, TR7 1BD.	0637 871345		21
*		*	Mr & Mrs Somerville, The Goose Rock Hotel, West Pentire, CRANTOCK. (£18.50)	0637 830755	774 607	22
*	*	*	Mrs Crofts, Tremore, Liskey Hill Crescent, PERRANPORTH. (£14.00)	0872 573537		23
*	*	*	Mrs M Saddler, Cellar Cove Hotel, Droskyn Way, PERRANPORTH, TR6 0DS. (£15.00)	0872 572110	752 543	23
*	*	*	B Terry, Park View Hotel, 42 Tywarnhayle Road, PERRANPORTH. (£11.00)	0872 573009		23
			Tourist Information Centre, Ponsmere Road, PERRANPORTH.	0872 573368		23

P	O	D	Name and Address	Telephone No.	Map Ref.	Section
*	*	*	Mrs J Ball, 15 Durning Road, ST AGNES, TR5 0UP. (£12.00)	0872 552532	717 502	24
*	*	*	Mrs Gill-Carey, Penkerris, Penwinnick Road, ST AGNES. (£13.50)	087255 2262	722 503	24
*	*	*	Mrs Glover, Beach Cottage, Quay Road, ST AGNES. (£13.00)	0872 553802		24
*	*	*	Mrs Treleaven, Driftwood Spars Hotel, Trevaunance Cove, ST AGNES, TR5 0RT. (£29.00)	0872 552428		24
*	*	*	Mrs G Van Leeuwen, Chy Todden, "Frying Dutchman", Quay Road, ST AGNES, TR5 0RY. (On cliff path) (£13.00)	0872 552664		24
*	*	*	Mrs Benson, Benson's, 1 The Hillside, PORTREATH, TR16 4LL. (£17.50)	0209 842534		26
*		*	Glenfeadon House Hotel, PORTREATH, TR16 4JV. (£18.00)	0209 842650		26
*	*	*	C J & J E Healan, Cliff House, The Square, PORTREATH, TR16 4LB. (£15.00)	0209 842008		26
*	*	*	Mr & Mrs R Pattinson, Sycamore Lodge, Primrose Terrace, PORTREATH, TR16 4JS. (£16.00)	0209 842784		26
*	*	*	Mrs M Symonds, Suhaili, 14 Forth-an-Nance, PORTREATH, TR16 4NQ. (£14.00)	0209 842110		26
*	*	*	Calize Country House, Prosper Hill, GWITHIAN, TR27 5BW. (£15.00)	0736 753268	589 409	27
*	*	*	Mr & Mrs D Eddy, Orchard Close, 3 Church Town Road, GWITHIAN. (£12.00)	0736 753077		27
*	*	*	Mrs A Cooper, 54 Penpol Terrace, HAYLE, TR27 4BQ. (£15.00)	0736 752855		27
*	*	*	White Hart Hotel, 10 Foundry Square, HAYLE, TR27 4HQ. (£29.50)	0736 752322		27
	*	*	Mr & Mrs W Batty, The Grey Mullet, 2 Bunkers Hill, ST IVES. (£15.00)	0736 796635		28
	*	*	Kandahar, 11 The Warren, ST IVES, TR26 2EA, (Town Centre). (£16.00)	0736 796183		28
*		*	Mrs King, Carlill, 9 Porthminster Terrace, ST IVES, TR26 2DQ. (£13.00)	0736 796738		28

P	O	D	Name and Address	Telephone No.	Map Ref.	Section
*	*	*	Mrs Millin, Lynmar, 4 The Terrace, ST IVES, TR26 2BL. (£12.00)	0736 794152		28
			Tourist Information Centre, The Guildhall, Street an Pol, ST IVES, TR26 2DT.	0736 796297		28
*	*	*	Mrs Berryman, Treen Farm, Gurnards Road, ZENNOR, St Ives, TR26 3DE. (£12.50)	0736 796932	436 377	29
*	*	*	Boswednack Manor, ZENNOR, St Ives, TR26 3DD. (£14.00)	0736 794183	442 377	29
*	*	*	N I Mann, Trewey Farm, ZENNOR, St Ives. (£14.00)	0736 796936	454 384	29
*	*	*	Pennance Farm, ZENNOR, St Ives. (£12.50)	0736 796972		29
*	*	*	Mrs A B Prowse, Trewey Vean Farm, ZENNOR, St Ives. (£13.00)	0736 796919		29
*	*	*	Mr & Mrs C Arms, The Old Smugglers Haunt Tea Rooms, PENDEEN, TR19 7SG. (£14.00)	0736 788310		29
	*	*	Mrs Bailey, Trewellard Manor Farm, PENDEEN. (£14.00)	0736 788526	375 339	29
*	*	*	Mrs B Brooke, Enys, Lighthouse Road, PENDEEN, Penzance, TR19 7ED. (£16.00)	0736 787143	380 358	29
*		*	Mr & Mrs T Dymond, The Old Count House, Boscaswell Down, PENDEEN, Near Penzance. (£13.00)	0736 788058		29
*	*	*	Mrs D. Jelbert, 1 Rose Valley, PENDEEN, Penzance, TR19 7TS. (£12.50)	0736 786244		29
	*		Mrs C Stone, 16 Levant Road, Trewellard, PENDEEN, TR19 7SU. (£10.00)	0736 787984		29
*	*	*	The Radjel Inn, PENDEEN, TR19 7DR. (£11.00)	0736 788446		29
	*	*	Mrs J Cargeeg, Manor Farm, BOTALLACK, TR19 7QG. (£14.00)	0736 788525	328 370	30
*	*	*	Boswedden House Hotel, Cape Cornwall, ST JUST, Penzance. (£17.00)	0736 788733	360 318	30
*		*	Mrs A D Eddy, Trethewes, Carrallack Terrace, ST JUST, Penzance, TR19 7LP. (£13.00)	0736 788528		30
*		*	Mr & Mrs J R Hartley, Bosavern House, ST JUST, Penzance, TR19 7RD. (£13.50)	0736 788301	371 305	30

P	O	D	Name and Address	Telephone No.	Map Ref.	Section
*		*	Mr & Mrs P Michelmore, 2 Fore Street, ST JUST, Nr Penzance. (£12.50)	0736 787784/910	371 313	30
	*	*	Mr & Mrs D Gallie, Polwyn Cottage, Old Coastguard Row, SENNEN COVE, TR19 7DA. (£13.50)	0736 871349	350 264	31
	*		A & A Rees, Myrtle Cottage, Old Coastguard Road, SENNEN COVE. (£12.50)	0736 871698		31
*	*	*	Mrs Flumm, Lyonesse Guest House, Land's End, SENNEN, TR19 7AD. (£12.50)	0736 871207	357 257	31
*	*	*	D Wedlake, Sennen Cove Hotel, Marias Lane, SENNEN, Near Penzance. (£16.00)	0736 871275		31

SOUTH CORNWALL

YOUTH HOSTELS PENZANCE, HELSTON, FALMOUTH, ST AUSTELL – SEE Y.H.A. SECTION PAGE

P	O	D	Name and Address	Telephone No.	Map Ref.	Section
*	*	*	Mr & Mrs P Christ, Sea View House, The Valley, PORTHCURNO, Penzance. (£13.00)	0736 810638		32
*	*	*	Mr & Mrs J Ring, Corniche, Trebehor, PORTHCURNO, TR19 6LX. (£12.00)	0736 871685	375 243 Will pick up	32
*	*	*	Mrs A Jilbert, Penver House Farm, Treen, ST LEVAN, Penzance. (£12.50)	0736 810778		33
*	*	*	Mr & Mrs B Richards, Tremeneth Hotel, LAMORNA, TR19 6XL. (£16.00)	0736 731367		33
*	*	*	Mrs Bartlett, Renovelle, 6 The Parade, MOUSEHOLE, Penzance, TR19 6PN. (£11.50)	0736 731258		34
*	*	*	The Lobster Pot, MOUSEHOLE, TR19 6QX. (£22.50)	0736 731251	469 263	34
*	*	*	Mrs G Ash, Torre Vene, Lescudjack Terrace, PENZANCE, TR18 3AE. (£13.00)	0736 64103		34
*	*	*	Miss R Knubley, Alexandra Hotel, Seafront, PENZANCE, TR18 4NX. (£23.50)	0736 62644/66333		34
*	*	*	Tarbert Hotel, Clarence Street, PENZANCE. (£22.50)	0736 63758		34
			Tourist Information Centre, Station Road, PENZANCE, TR18 2NF.	0736 62207		34
*	*	*	Mrs I S Glover, Anneth Lowen, Leys Lane, MARAZION, Cornwall. (£12.00)	0736 710211		35
*	*	*	Mrs M Foy, Mzima, Penlee Close, PRAA SANDS. (£11.00)	0736 763856		36

P	O	D	Name and Address	Telephone No.	Map Ref.	Section
*	*	*	Mrs Jennings, Boslowen-Mor, Castle Drive, PRAA SANDS, TR20 9TF. (£12.00)	0736 762223		36
*	*	*	Mrs C Cookson, Pentre, Peverell Terrace, PORTHLEVEN, TR13 9DZ. (£14.00)	0326 574493	630 255	37
*	*	*	Mrs K Cox, Quayside Cottage, 12 Harbour View, PORTHLEVEN, TR13 9JN. (£15.00)	0326 562200		37
*	*	*	Mr Hallam, Seefar, Peverell Terrace, PORTHLEVEN. (£12.00)	0326 573778		37
*	*	*	Mrs P Jewson, Vilvorde, Breageside, PORTHLEVEN, TR13 7JT. (£15.00)	0326 564294		37
*		*	Ms M Kelymack, An Modros Hotel, Peverell Terrace, PORTHLEVEN, TR13 9BZ. (£16.00)	0326 562236		37
	*	*	Robin Minshall, Ring o'Bright Water, Loe Bar Road, PORTHLEVEN, Helston. (£12.50)	0326 564765		37
*	*	*	Tye Rock Hotel, Loe Bar Road, PORTHLEVEN, TR13 9EW. (£25.00)	0326 572695		37
*		*	S A Archer, Redannack Bungalow, Lender Lane, MULLION, TR12 7HS. (£13.00)	0326 240936		38
*	*	*	Mrs I Clarke, Trematon, Polurrian, Cliff Road, MULLION, TR12 7EW. (£12.50) (on the path)	0326 240344		38
*	*	*	Mrs C Harry, Westward, Lender Lane, MULLION, TR12 7HW. (£14.00)	0326 240950		38
*		*	Mullion Cove Hotel, MULLION, TR12 7EP. (£26.00)	0326 240328		38
*	*	*	Pauline Story, Criggan Mill, MULLION COVE, TR12 7EU. (£12.50)	0326 240496	671 178	38
*	*	*	Mr S Crossley, Mounts Bay House Hotel, Penmenner Road, THE LIZARD, TR12 7NP. (£17.50)	0326 290305		39
		*	Mrs P Hocking, Bayview, Cross Common, THE LIZARD, Helston, TR12 7PD. (£12.50)	0326 290369	707 126	39
*		*	Mr & Mrs S Kilmister, Parc Brawse House, Penmenner Road, THE LIZARD, Helston, TR12 7NR. (£12.50)	0326 290466	702 122	39
		*	Mrs G Rowe, Trethvas Farm, THE LIZARD, Helston, TR12 7AR. (£13.00)	0326 290720	709 136	39
*	*	*	Mrs K Thirlaway, Green Cottage, THE LIZARD, TR12 7NZ. (£11.50)	0326 290099		39

P	O	D	Name and Address	Telephone No.	Map Ref.	Section
*	*	*	Caerthillian Farmhouse, LIZARD, Near Helston, TR12 7NX. (£13.50)	0326 290596		39
*	*	*	Mrs I Sowden, The Most Southerly House, LIZARD POINT, TR12 7NU. (£12.00)	0326 290300	702 115	39
*	*	*	Mrs A Betty, High Massetts, CADGWITH, Helston, TR12 7LA. (£15.60)	0326 290571		40
*	*	*	Cadgwith Hotel, CADGWITH, Near Helston. (£17.50)	0326 290513		40
*		*	Mrs L Johnson, Moorlands, Prazegooth Lane, CADGWITH, Nr Helston, TR12 7LB. (£15.00)	0326 290932		40
*		*	Mrs T Carey, Tamarisk Cottage, COVERACK, Helston. (£13.00)	0326 280638		40
*	*	*	Mr P Cheze-Brown, The Croft, North Corner, COVERACK, TR12 6TF. (£13.50)	0326 280387	783 187	40
*	*	*	Mrs E Daw, Bakery Cottage, COVERACK, Nr Helston. (£13.00)	0326 280474		40
*	*	*	Gallen-Treath Guest House, PORTHALLOW, St Keverne. (£17.00)	0326 280400		41
*	*	*	Mrs P Julian, Landrivick Farm, MANACCAN, Near Helston. (£16.00)	0326 231249		41
*		*	Tregildry Hotel, Gillan, MANACCAN, Near Helston, TR12 6HG. (£26.00)	0326 231378		41
*	*	*	Mrs J Chambers, Heronsway, Orchard Lane, HELFORD, TR12 6LA. (£15.00)	0326 231424	755 260	41
	*	*	J Davies, Pengwedhen, HELFORD, Helston. (£12.50)	0326 231481	755 263	41
*	*	*	Mrs Spike, Carwinion Vean, Grove Hill, MAWNAN SMITH, Near Falmouth, TR11 5ER. (£16.50)	0326 250513		42
*	*	*	Dr & Mrs K G Leach, St Petrock, The Avenue, TRURO, TR1 1HR. (£13.00) (will pick up from and return to coast path)	0872 70768		42
*	*	*	Mrs Bryant, Ambleside, 9 Marlborough Road, FALMOUTH, TR11 3LP. (£14.00)	0326 319630		42
*		*	D & M Siderfin, Bradgate Guest House, 4 Florence, Place FALMOUTH. (£14.00)	0326 314108		42

P	O	D	Name and Address	Telephone No.	Map Ref.	Section
*	*	*	The Grove Hotel, Grove Place, FALMOUTH, TR11 4AV. (£20.00)	0326 319577		42
*		*	Mrs Watmore, Rosemary Hotel, Gyllyngvase Terrace, FALMOUTH. (£15.00)	0326 314669	810 318	42
			Tourist Information Centre 28 Killigrew Street, FALMOUTH, TR11 3PN.	0326 312300		42
		*	Braganza, Grove Hill, ST MAWES. (£18.00)	0326 270281	847 333	43
*	*	*	Penhallow Coombe Farm, Treworlas, Ruan High Lanes, ST MAWES. (£12.00)	0872 501105		43
*		*	M J Davis, Harberton House, Churchtown Road, Gerrans, PORTSCATHO, TR2 5DZ. (£15.00)	0872 580598		44
*	*	*	Mrs J Hickley, 40 Churchtown Road, Gerrans, PORTSCATHO, TR2 5DY. (£17.50)	0872 580389		44
*	*	*	Mr & Mrs R Pooler, Tregerein Guest House, PORTSCATHO, TR2 5HT. (£14.00)	0872 580336		44
	*	*	Mrs J Smith, 4 Parc An Dillon, PORTSCATHO, TR2 5DU. (£16.00)	0872 580310		44
*	*	*	Mrs A Palmer, Trenestrall Farm, Philleigh, Ruan High Lanes, PORTSCATHO. (£12.00) (will pick up from path)	0872 501259	886 399	44
*	*	*	Mr & Mrs R Foley, St Petroc, PORTLOE, TR2 5RA. (£12.50)	0872 501143		45
*	*	*	Mrs C Holdsworth, Tregain Tea Room, The Post Office, PORTLOE, Truro, TR2 5QU. (£16.50)	0872 501252		45
*	*	*	Mr J H Gregory, Llawnroc Inn, GORRAN HAVEN, PL26 6NU. (£16.00)	0726 843461		47
*	*	*	Gill Mott, Piggy Pantry, The Willows, GORRAN HAVEN, ST AUSTELL. (£14.00)	0726 843545		47
*	*	*	Mr & Mrs D Youlden, Steep House, Portmellon Cove, MEVAGISSEY, PL26 6TQ. (£15.00)	0726 843732	441 017	48
*	*	*	Ms J Connolly, Mandalay Hotel, School Hill, MEVAGISSEY, PL26 6TQ. (£15.00)	0726 842435		48
*	*	*	Mrs Hugh, Polvellan School Hill, MEVAGISSEY, PL26 6TG. (£16.00)	0726 842197		48
*	*	*	A H Lawrence, Tregoron Guest House, Cliff Street, MEVAGISSEY, PL26 6QW. (£14.00)	0726 842319	016 441	48

P	O	D	Name and Address	Telephone No.	Map Ref.	Section
*		*	Mrs J Rowe, Rosedale, Valley Park, Tregoney Hill, MEVAGISSEY, PL26 6RS. (£14.00)	0726 842769		48
*	*	*	Mrs M Bainbridge, Polrudden Farm, PENTEWAN, PL26 6BJ. (£12.50)	0726 843213	025 475	48
*	*	*	Mr I Christie, T'Gallants Guest House, 6 Charlestown Road, CHARLESTOWN, PL25 3NJ. (£25.00)	0726 70203		49
*	*	*	Porth Avallen Hotel, Sea Road, Carlyon Bay, CHARLESTOWN, Near St Austell. (£35.00)	0726 812802		49
	*	*	Mrs B D Burgess, 55 Polmear Road, PAR, PL24 2AW. (£10.00)	0726 812967	086 535	50
*	*	*	Mr R Blount, Countrywide Holidays, Fowey Hall, Hanson Drive, FOWEY, PL23 1ET. (£15.00)	0726 833104	122 516	51
*	*	*	Mrs J Rowledge, Trevanion Guest House, 70 Lostwithiel Street, FOWEY, PL23 1BQ. (£14.50)	0726 832602		51
*		*	Mr & Mrs D Turner, Topsides, The Esplanade, FOWEY, PL23 1HZ. (£14.00)	0726 833715	124 516	51
			Tourist Information Centre, The Post Office, 4 Custom House Hill, FOWEY, PL23 1AA.	0726 833616		51
*	*	*	Mrs B Blamey, Holly House, Fore Street, POLRUAN. (£13.50)	0726 870478		52
*	*	*	Mrs P Moore, Chyavallon, Landaviddy Lane, POLPERRO, PL13 2RT. (£14.00) Centre of village	0503 72788		52
*	*	*	Mrs C Talling, Lansallos Barton Farm, Lansallos, POLPERRO, PL13 2PU. (£12.00)	0503 72192		52
*	*	*	Mr & Mrs R Hill, 43 Tregarrick, The Downs, WEST LOOE, PL13 2SD. (£11.50)	0503 262652		53
*	*	*	Mr M Neaves, Schooner Point, 1 Trelawney Terrace, WEST LOOE, PL13 2AG. (£13.00)	0503 262670		53
			Tourist Information Centre, The Guildhall, Fore Street, LOOE, PL13 1AA.	0503 262072		53
*	*	*	Mr J Chapman, Woodlands, St Martins Road, EAST LOOE, PL13 1LP. (£18.00)	0503 264405	251 541	53
*	*	*	Marwinthy Guest House, East Cliff, EAST LOOE, PL13 1DE. (£15.00)	0503 264382	256 533	53

P	O	D	Name and Address	Telephone No.	Map Ref.	Section
*		*	Mrs A J Harvey, The Bungalow, Cliff Road, CRAFTHOLE, Nr Torpoint, PL11 3BY. (£15.00)	0503 30334	355 541	54
*	*	*	C Collins, Avon House, Garrett Street, CAWSAND, PL10 1DB. (£11.00)	0752 822229	435 503	55
*	*	*	Mr & Mrs A Fidler, Rame Barton, Rame, CAWSAND, Near Torpoint, PL10 1LG. (£15.00)	0752 822789	425 492	55
*	*	*	Mrs D Goodwright, Clarendon, Garrett Street, CAWSAND, PL10 1PD. (£13.00)	0752 823460		55
*	*	*	Halfway House Inn, Fore Street, Cawsand Bay, KINGSAND, PL10 1NA. (£18.50)	0752 822279	435 505	55

SOUTH DEVON

YOUTH HOSTELS PLYMOUTH, BRIXHAM, SEATON – SEE Y.H.A. SECTION PAGE

There are many B & B establishments in the West Hoe Area of Plymouth virtually on the Coast Path.

P	O	D	Name and Address	Telephone No.	Map Ref.	Section
*	*	*	Ms A Coon, Berkeley's Guest House, 4 St James Place East, The Hoe, PLYMOUTH, Devon. (£15.00)	0752 221654		56
*	*	*	Kynance Hotel, 107/113 Citadel Road, The Hoe, PLYMOUTH, PL1 2RN. (£16.00)	0752 266821	544 481	56
*	*	*	Mr & Mrs M H Preece, Rigsbys, 35 North Road East, PLYMOUTH, PL4 6AY. (£13.50)	0752 669161		56
			Tourist Information Centre, Civic Centre, PLYMOUTH, PL1 2EW.	0752 264849/264851		56
*	*	*	Mr & Mrs J Pascho, Pyne Villa, Yonder Street, HOOE, Nr Plymouth, PL9 9RB. (£13.00)	0752 403368		56
*	*	*	Mrs Janet Rayne, The Boringdon Arms, TURNCHAPEL, Plymouth, PL9 9TQ. (£14.00)	0752 402053		56
*	*	*	Heybrook Bay Private Hotel, Beach Road, HEYBROOK BAY, Near Plymouth, PL9 0BS. (£16.00)	0752 862345		57
*	*	*	Mrs J Cross, Maywood Cottage, Bridgend, NEWTON FERRERS, PL8 1AW. (£15.00)	0752 872372	555 487	58
*	*	*	Mrs Johnson, Crown Yealm, NEWTON FERRERS. (£16.00)	0752 872365		58
*	*	*	River Yealm Hotel, Yealm Road, NEWTON FERRERS, PL8 1BL. (£30.00)	0752 872419		58

P	O	D	Name and Address	Telephone No.	Map Ref.	Section
*	*	*	Mrs L A Brunning, Netton Farm House, NOSS MAYO, PL8 1HA. (£16.50) (will pick up)	0752 873080	537 471	58
*	*	*	Mr F A Gregory, Little Lawford Cottage, Bridgend, NOSS MAYO, PL8 1DX. (£12.50)	0752 872521	554 478	58
*	*	*	Mrs A Hill, Rowden House, Stoke Road, NOSS MAYO, PL8 1JG. (£13.50)	0752 872153	555 471	58
*	*	*	Mr Steer, Rookery Nook, Hannaford, NOSS MAYO. (£15.00)	0752 872296		58
*	*	*	Mrs Pearse, Scobbiscombe Farm, HOLBETON, Near Yealmpton, PL8 2EW. (£12.00)	075530 275		58
*	*	*	Mrs E Wallis, Windlestraw, Penquit, ERMINGTON, PL21 0LU. (£15.00) (Will pick up and return from Yealm, Erme and Avon estuaries)	0752 896237	646 544	57/58
*	*	*	Mr N Kies, Torr House, KINGSTON, Kingsbridge, TQ7 4PT. (£15.00)	0548 810723	640 480	58
*	*	*	D R Kinder, Trebles Cottage Hotel, KINGSTON, TQ7 4PT. (£23.00)	0548 810268	640 480	58
*	*	*	Mrs P Brunskill, Cliff Path, RINGMORE, Kingsbridge, TQ7 4HR. (£13.00)	0548 810654	651 456	58
*	*	*	Mrs I Dodds, Ayrmer House, RINGMORE, Near Kingsbridge. (£16.00)	0548 810391		58
*	*	*	Journey's End Inn, RINGMORE, TQ7 4HL. (£20.00)	0548 810205		58
*	*	*	Mrs B Evans, Merrylees, Ringmore Drive, BIGBURY ON SEA, TQ7 4AU. (£15.00)	0548 810247		58
*	*	*	Mr & Mrs G Fortune, The Kashu, Cleveland Drive, BIGBURY, TQ7 4AX. (£15.00)	0548 810584		58
*	*	*	Mrs B Lee, Rosebank, Folly Hill, BIGBURY-ON -SEA, TQ7 4AR. (£17.00)	0548 810724	653 444	58
*	*	*	Mr M Scatterfield, Henley Hotel, Folly Hill, BIGBURY-ON-SEA, TQ7 4AR. (£16.00)	0548 810240/331	657 444	58
*	*	*	Mr & Mrs J A Parrish, Higher Barnfield, Fore Street, KINGSBRIDGE, TQ7 1AX. (£15.00)	0548 853332	734 448	58/59/60
*	*	*	Mr P J Sanders, Heron House Hotel, Thurlestone Sands, Near HOPE COVE. (£20.00)	0548 561308/600	676 412	59
*	*	*	Mr & Mrs N Upsdale, La Mer Hotel, Thurlestone Sands, Near HOPE COVE, TQ7 3JY. (On the path). (£13.00)	0548 561207	675 412	59

P	O	D	Name and Address	Telephone No.	Map Ref.	Section
*	*	*	Mr & Mrs W Hewitt, Rockcliffe, Outer Hope Cove, HOPE COVE, TQ7 3HG. (£15.50)	0548 560061		59
*	*	*	Mrs G Idris, May Villa, Inner Hope Cove, HOPE COVE, Near Kingsbridge, TQ7 3HP. (£14.00)	0548 561887		59
*	*	*	Mr & Mrs R Petty-Brown, Rocarno, Grenville Road, SALCOMBE, TQ8 8BJ. (£12.50)	0548 842732	735 389	60
*	*	*	Mr & Mrs Axtell, Amalfi, Grenville Road, SALCOMBE. (£12.00)	0548 842155		60
*	*	*	Lyndhurst Hotel, Bonaventure Road,, SALCOMBE, TQ8 8BG. (£19.50)	0548 842481		60
*		*	Terrapins Hotel, Buckley, SALCOMBE, TQ8 8DD. (£23.95)	0548 842861		60
*	*	*	The Lodge, Devon Road, SALCOMBE, TQ8 8HL. (£12.50)	0548 844008		60
*		*	Torre View Hotel, Devon Road, SALCOMBE, TQ8 8HJ. (£21.00)	0548 842633	735 385	60
			Tourist Information Centre, Council Hall, Market Street, SALCOMBE, TQ8 8QL.	0548 842736		60
*	*	*	A & M Catt, Migrants Rest, EAST PRAWLE, Near Kingsbridge, TQ7 2DB. (£13.00)	0548 51443	779 366	61
*		*	M & L Davies, Maelcombe House, EAST PRAWLE, TQ7 2DE. (£17.62)	054851 300	791 364	61
*		*	Mr & Mrs D Morris, Hines Hill, EAST PRAWLE, TQ7 2BZ. (£18.00)	054851 263	784 363	61
*	*	*	Hallsands, Hotel, Hallsands, TORCROSS, TQ7 2EY. (£17.50)	0548 51264	818 388	61
*	*	*	Mrs V J Mercer, Old Walls, Slapton, TORCROSS, TQ7 2QN. (£13.50)	0548 580516	822 449	61
*		*	Jan Urmson, Waterside, Slapton Sands, TORCROSS. (£14.00)	0548 580280		61
*	*	*	L Nixon, Southfield House, STOKE FLEMING, Dartmouth, TQ6 0NR. (£17.50)	0803 770359		61
*	*	*	E A Hayes, 2 Charles Street, DARTMOUTH, TQ6 9QG. (£13.00)	0803 833823	Central Dartmouth	62
*	*	*	Mr & Mrs K Johnston, Capritia, 69 Victoria Road, DARTMOUTH, TQ6 9RX. (£15.00)	0803 833419		62

P	O	D	Name and Address	Telephone No.	Map Ref.	Section
			Tourist Information Centre, Newcomen Engine House, Major's Avenue, DARTMOUTH, TQ6 9YY.	0803 834224		62
*	*	*	Carlton House, Higher Street, KINGSWEAR, TQ6 0AG. (£13.00)	0803 752244		63
*		*	Sampford House, 57/59 King Street, BRIXHAM, TQ5 9TH. (£14.00)	0803 857761		63
*	*	*	Mrs L J Snowden, Richmond House, Higher Manor Road, BRIXHAM, TQ5 8HA. (£16.00)	0803 882391	921 561	63
*		*	Mrs N Doling, Woodlands Guest House, Parkham Road, BRIXHAM, TQ5 9BU. (£18.00)	0803 852040	923 559	63
			Tourist Information Centre, The Quay, BRIXHAM, TQ5 8TB.	0803 852861		63
*		*	Mrs J Ford, Bou-Saada Private Hotel, 62A Osney Crescent, PAIGNTON, TQ4 5EZ. (£12.75)	0803 551158		64
*		*	Mrs P Kingdom, Bruce Lodge Guest House, 2 Elmsleigh Road, PAIGNTON, TQ4 5AU. (£12.00)	0803 550972		64
*	*	*	Mrs M McHolm, 5a Fortescue Road, PAIGNTON, TQ3 3BZ. (£10.00)	0803 550667	894 616	64
*	*	*	Mrs P Whitlam, Cheltor Hotel, 20 St Andrews Road, PAIGNTON, TQ4 6HA. (£12.00)	0803 551507	891 602	64
			Tourist Information Centre, Festival Hall, Esplanade Road, PAIGNTON.	0803 558383		64
	*	*	Mrs Sibthorpe, The Beehive, Sheep Hill, Maidencombe, TORQUAY, TQ1 4TS. (£15.00)	0803 314647		64
			Tourist Information Centre, Vaughan Parade, TORQUAY	0803 297428		64
*	*	*	Glenside Hotel, Ringmore Road, SHALDON. (£17.50)	0626 872448		65
			Tourist Information Centre, The Den, TEIGNMOUTH, TQ14 8BE.	0626 779769		66
*		*	Mr & Mrs D Badcock, West Hatch Hotel, 34 West Cliff, DAWLISH, EX7 9DN. (£17.00)	0626 864211		66
*	*	*	Mrs M Crouch, Glendora, Hall Lane, Holcombe, DAWLISH, EX7 0JP. (£15.00)	0626 864119	954 748	66
			Tourist Information Centre, The Lawn, DAWLISH, EX7 9AP.	0626 863589		66
*	*	*	Barn Hotel, Foxholes Hill, EXMOUTH, EX8 2DF. (£32.00)	0395 224411		66

P	O	D	Name and Address	Telephone No.	Map Ref.	Section
*	*	*	Mrs P Garwood, St Aubyns Guest House, 11 Hartley Road, EXMOUTH, EX8 2SG. (£14.50)	0395 264069		66
*		*	Mrs Shobrook, 30 Withycombe Road, EXMOUTH, EX8 1TG. (£12.50)	0395 277025		66
			Tourist Information Centre, Alexandra Terrace, EXMOUTH, EX8 1NZ.	0395 263744		66
		*	Mrs Fletcher, The White Cottage, 25 East Budleigh Road, BUDLEIGH SALTERTON, EX9 6EJ. (£15.00)	0395 443574		67
*		*	Mrs J Franklin, 2 Warren Drive, BUDLEIGH SALTERTON, EX9 6EL. (£17.00)	0395 445690		67
*	*	*	Mrs S Freeman, 10 Knowle Village, BUDLEIGH SALTERTON. (£14.00)	0395 445807	050 825	67
*	*	*	J Lee, Chapter House, 6 Westbourne Terrace, BUDLEIGH SALTERTON, EX9 6BR. (£13.50)	0395 444100		67
*	*	*	Mrs Shaw, 7 Otter Court, Stoneborough Lane, BUDLEIGH SALTERTON, EX9 6JH. (£14.00)	0395 446384	071 822	67
			Tourist Information Centre, Fore Street, BUDLEIGH SALTERTON, EX9 6NG.	0395 445275		67
*	*	*	Diana Lee, Cheriton Guest House, 1 Elysian Villas, Vicarage Road, SIDMOUTH. (£12.00)	0395 513810		68
*		*	Mrs L Lever, Canterbury House, Salcombe Road, SIDMOUTH, EX10 8PR. (£16.00)	0395 513373		68
			Tourist Information Centre, Ham Lane, SIDMOUTH, EX10 8XR.	0395 516441		68
*	*	*	The Dolphin Hotel, Fore Street, BEER, EX12 3EQ. (£14.00)	0297 20068		69
*	*	*	Mr & Mrs R Hart, Hole Mill, Branscombe, SEATON, EX12 3BX.	0297 80314	193 895	69
*	*	*	Tors Guest House, 55 Harbour Road, SEATON, EX12 2LX. (£16.00)	0297 20531		69
			Tourist Information Centre (Seasonal), The Esplanade, SEATON.	0297 21689		69

DORSET

P	O	D	Name and Address	Telephone No.	Map Ref.	Section
*	*	*	Mrs & Mrs T Fuller, Old Monmouth Hotel, 12 Church Street, LYME REGIS, DT7 3BS. (£16.00)	0297 442456		70

P	O	D	Name and Address	Telephone No.	Map Ref.	Section
*		*	Mrs J Harding, Coverdale Guest House, Woodmead Road, LYME REGIS. (£11.00)	0297 442882		70
			Tourist Information Centre, Guildhall Cottage, Church Street, LYME REGIS, DT7 3QA.	0297 442138		70
*	*	*	Mr & Mrs P A Charge, Charleston House, The Street, CHARMOUTH, DT6 6NX. (£12.50)	0297 60347	362 938	71
*	*	*	Thatch Lodge, The Street, CHARMOUTH, DT6 6PQ. (£17.00)	0297 60407	364 936	71
*	*	*	Mrs M Ward, Springfield House, Axminster Road, CHARMOUTH, DT6 6PB. (£15.00)	0297 60509	361 937	71
*	*	*	Mr K A Baylis, Seatown Cottage, SEATOWN, Chideock, Bridport, DT6 6JT. (£13.00)	0297 89027	420 919	72
*	*	*	S Herring, Sea Braes, Third Cliff Walk, WEST BAY, Bridport, DT6 4HJ. (£14.00)	0308 23536	458 906	72
*	*	*	Mrs V Vallard, Egdon, Third Cliff Walk, WEST BAY, DT6 4HX. (£12.50)	0308 22542	456 907	72
*	*	*	Mrs D Loving, 144 West Bay Road, BRIDPORT, DT6 4AZ. (£14.00)	0308 22577		72
*	*	*	Tourist Information Centre, 32 South Street, BRIDPORT, DT6 3NO.	0309 24901		71
*	*	*	Mrs S A Andrews, Foxbarrow House, LANGSTON HERRING, Weymouth, DT3 4HT. (£15.00)	0305 871463	614 825	74
*	*	*	Mrs J Baker, Aveswood, 5 Bramdon Lane, Portesham, WEYMOUTH. (£15.00)	0305 871413	603 856	74
*	*	*	Mr & Mrs D J Boucher, Southbrook, Preston Road, Overcombe, WEYMOUTH, DT3 6PU. (£16.00)	0305 832208		74
	*	*	Mrs M Wakefield, Anchorage, 23 Stavordale Road, WEYMOUTH, DT4 0AB. (£14.00)	0305 785719	675 792	74
*	*	*	Mr & Mrs G Wincott, Florian, 59 Abbotsbury Road, Westham, WEYMOUTH, DT4 0AQ. (£16.00)	0305 773836		74
			Tourist Information Centre, The Esplanade, WEYMOUTH, DT4 8ED.	0305 785747		74
	*	*	Mrs K Legg, Rosedale, Church Lane, OSMINGTON, Near Weymouth, DT3 6EW. (£13.00)	0305 832056		75
*	*	*	Ms B Leigh, Rosthwaite, Church Lane, OSMINGTON, DT3 6EW. (£13.00)	0305 833621		75
*	*	*	Mrs C Hemsley, Botany Farm, Wareham Road, EAST LULWORTH Dorset BH20 5QH. (£15.00)	0929 41427	868 827 will pick up	75

P	O	D	Name and Address	Telephone No.	Map Ref.	Section
*	*	*	R & D Foote, Lulworth Cove Hotel, WEST LULWORTH, Wareham, BH20 5RQ. (£18.00)	0929 41333	on the path	75
*		*	Shirley Hotel, WEST LULWORTH, Wareham, BH20 5RL. (£21.60)	0929 41358	824 806	75
*	*	*	P & L Simpson, Newland Farm, WEST LULWORTH, Wareham. (£18.00)	092941 376	810 810	75
*	*	*	Mrs A Hole, Kimmeridge Farm House, KIMMERIDGE, West Lulworth, BH20 5PE. (£16.00)	0929 480990		76
*	*	*	Mrs G Hole, Bradle Farm, Church Knowle, KIMMERIDGE, BH20 5NU. (£15.50)	0929 480712	930 805	76
		*	Mr & Mrs A Preston, The Corner House, 4 Manor Road, SWANAGE, BH19 2BJ. (£13.00)	0929 424410		77
	*	*	Esme Prior, Belros, Worth Matravers, SWANAGE. (£17.00)	0929 439259		77
*	*	*	Sea Glimpse, 2 Stafford Road, SWANAGE. (£15.00)	0929 425035		77
*		*	Skelmorlie House, 50 Queens Road, SWANAGE, BH19 2EU. (£14.50)	0929 424643	031 784	77
*		*	Mrs B Willey, Verulam Lodge, 26 Cluny Crescent, SWANAGE, BH19 2BT. (£14.00)	0929 422079		77
			Tourist Information Centre, The White House, Shore Road, SWANAGE, BH19 1LB.	0929 422885		77
*	*	*.	Mrs North, The Laurels, 60 Britannia Road, POOLE, BH14 8BB. (£16.00)	0202 723369		78
			Tourist Information Centre, The Quay, POOLE, BH15 1HE.	0202 673322		78

YOUTH HOSTEL ASSOCIATION – ACCOMMODATION ADDRESSES

There is an amazing variety of Youth Hostels along the South West Way, 25 in total and all offering comfortable, friendly accommodation. Prices start from £3.50 per night including bed linen, the use of self-catering kitchens, drying rooms and cycle sheds. The YHA is a membership organisation, non members are welcome to join on arrival at the Youth Hostel. Membership (annual £3 Under 18 – £9 Adult) enables you to take advantage of the 5000 Youth Hostels world wide, regular member's magazine 'Triangle', annual YHA Accommodation Guides and discounts at YHA Adventure Shops and local tourist attractions. The meals are excellent value, Breakfast £2.60, Packed Lunch £2.10–£2.90, Evening Meal £3.90.

Book directly with the Youth Hostel of your choice or for further assistance please contact South England Regional Office, 11b York Road, Salisbury, Wiltshire, SP2 7AP. Tel: 0722-337494.

Prices range from £3.50 to £8.70 and are for bed only, available on application to each Hostel.

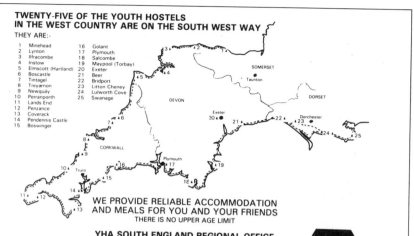

TWENTY-FIVE OF THE YOUTH HOSTELS
IN THE WEST COUNTRY ARE ON THE SOUTH WEST WAY
THEY ARE:-

1	Minehead	16	Golant
2	Lynton	17	Plymouth
3	Ilfracombe	18	Salcombe
4	Instow	19	Maypool (Torbay)
5	Elmscott (Hartland)	20	Exeter
6	Boscastle	21	Beer
7	Tintagel	22	Bridport
8	Treyarnon	23	Litton Cheney
9	Newquay	24	Lulworth Cove
10	Perranporth	25	Swanage
11	Lands End		
12	Penzance		
13	Coverack		
14	Pendennis Castle		
15	Boswinger		

WE PROVIDE RELIABLE ACCOMMODATION
AND MEALS FOR YOU AND YOUR FRIENDS
THERE IS NO UPPER AGE LIMIT

YHA SOUTH ENGLAND REGIONAL OFFICE
11B YORK ROAD, SALISBURY, WILTSHIRE, SP2 7AP.
Telephone. (0722) 337494

P	O	D	Name and Address	Telephone No.	Map Ref.	Section
			SOMERSET			
*	*		Minehead Youth Hostel, Alcombe Combe, Minehead, TA24 6EW	Minehead (0643) 702595	973 442	1
			NORTH DEVON			
*	*		Lynton Youth Hostel, Lynbridge, Lynton, EX35 6AZ.	Lynton (0598) 53237	720 487	2
*	*		Ilfracombe Youth Hostel, Ashmour House, 1 Hillsborough Tce., Ilfracombe, EX34 9NR.	Ilfracombe (0271) 65337	524 476	4
*	*		Instow Youth Hostel, Worlington House, New Road, Instow, Bideford, EX39 4LW.	Instow (0271) 860394	482 303	9
	*		Elmscott Youth Hostel, Hartland, Bideford, EX39 6ES. (Self catering only.)	Hartland (0237) 441367	231 217	11
			CORNWALL			
*	*		Boscastle Youth Hostel, Palace Stables, Boscastle, PL35 0HD.	Boscastle (08405) 287 or (0840) 250287	096 915	14
	*		Tintagel Youth Hostel, Dunderhole Point, Tintagel, PL34 0DW. (Self catering only)	Tintagel (0840) 770334	047 881	15
	*		Treyarnon Youth Hostel, Tregonnan, Treyarnon, Padstow PL28 8JR.	Padstow (0841) 520322	859 741	19
*	*		Newquay Youth Hostel, Alexandra Court, Narrowcliff, Newquay, TR7 2QF.	Newquay (0637) 876381	818 619	21

(This hostel is for sale and may not be available throughout 1994. Check beforehand).

P	O	D	Name and Address	Telephone No.	Map Ref.	Section
		*	Perranporth, Youth Hostel, Droskyn Point, Perranporth, TR6 0DS. (Self catering only)	Truro (0872) 573812	752 544	23
*		*	Land's End Youth Hostel, Letcha Vean, St Just-in-Penwith, Penzance, TR19 7NT.	Penzance (0736) 788437	364 305	30
*		*	Penzance Youth Hostel, Castle Horneck, Alverton, Penzance, TR20 8TF.	Penzance (0736) 62666	457 302	34
*		*	Coverack Youth Hostel, Parc Behan, School Hill, Coverack, Helston, TR12 6SA.	St Keverne (0326) 280687	782 181	40
*		*	Pendennis Castle Youth Hostel, Pendennis Castle, Falmouth, TR11 4LP.	Falmouth (0326) 311435	823 319	42
*		*	Boswinger Youth Hostel, Boswinger, Gorran, St Austell, PL26 6LL.	Mevagissey (0726) 843234	991 411	49
*		*	Golant Youth Hostel, Penquite House, Golant, Fowey, PL23 1LA	Fowey (0726) 833507	118 557	51

SOUTH DEVON

P	O	D	Name and Address	Telephone No.	Map Ref.	Section
*		*	Plymouth Youth Hostel, Belmont House, Devonport Road, Stoke,. Plymouth, PL3 4DW.	Plymouth (0752) 562189	461 555	55
*		*	Salcombe Youth Hostel, 'Overbecks', Sharpitor, Salcombe, TQ8 8LW.	Salcombe (054884) 2856	728 374	60
*		*	Maypool Youth Hostel, Maypool House, Galmpton, Brixham, TQ5 0ET.	Churston (0803) 842444	877 546	64
*		*	Exeter Youth Hostel, 47–49 Countess Wear Road, Exeter, EX2 6LR	Exeter (0392) 876939	942 897	66/67
*		*	Beer Youth Hostel, Bovey Combe, Townsend, Beer, Seaton, EX12 3LL.	Seaton (0297) 20296	223 896	69

DORSET

P	O	D	Name and Address	Telephone No.	Map Ref.	Section
*		*	Bridport Youth Hostel, West Rivers House, West Allington, Bridport, DT6 5BW.	Bridport (0308) 22655	461 930	72
*		*	Litton Cheney Youth Hostel, Litton Cheney, Dorchester, DT2 9AT. (No smoking hostel.)	Long Bredy (0308) 482340	548 900	74
*		*	Lulworth Cove Youth Hostel, School Lane, West Lulworth, Wareham, BH20 5SA.	W. Lulworth (0929) 400564	832 806	75
*		*	Swanage Youth Hostel, Cluny, Cluny Cresc., Swanage, BH19 2BS.	Swanage (0929) 422113	030 785	77

CAMPING

A list of Camp Sites has been prepared in path order anti-clockwise. Useful information and free leaflets can also be obtained as follows:

The Exmoor Visitor 1992: A free comprehensive guide (including accommodation). Please apply to Department E.V., Exmoor National Park Authority, Exmoor House, Dulverton, Somerset TA22 9HL.

Tourist Officer, Cornwall County Council, County Hall, Truro.

Devon County Tourist Officer, County Hall, Topsham Road, Exeter.

County Public Relations & Information Officer, County Hall, Dorchester, Dorset DT1 1XJ.

Individuals – but we stress **not parties** – usually find no problem in obtaining leave to camp away from official camp sites if they request permission to do so. In fact, our correspondence has many examples of extra kindnesses extended by farmers and others to campers. We would, however, very much emphasize the requesting of permission first. It would be so easy for the thoughtlessness of a few to undo the good relationships of many others built up over some years.

This list is thin in many areas. Suggestions for inclusions in future lists will always be welcome. Information of any new sites should be addressed to the Membership Secretary.

Name and Address	Telephone No.	Map Ref.	Site Open (Dates inclusive)	Section
NORTH DEVON				
Newberry Campsite, Woodlands, COMBE MARTIN, EX34 0AT.	0271 882333/4	576 473	Easter – October	3
Hele Valley Holiday Park, Hele Bay, ILFRACOMBE, EX34 9RD.	0271 862460		April – October	4
Croyde Bay Holidays, Croyde Bay, Moore Lane, CROYDE, Nr Braunton, EX33 1NZ.	0271 890351	395 437	Easter – October	7
Mr G J Reynolds, Pusehill Farm, Buckleigh, WESTWARD HO! EX39 5AH.	0237 474295	427 283	Easter – September	9
Mrs J Johns, Dyke Green Farm Camping Site, HIGHER CLOVELLY, Bideford, EX39 5RU.	0237 431279/699		Easter – October	10
Mr George, Downe Farm, HARTLAND, Devon.	0237 441210	237 247	All year	11
C J Davey, Stoke Barton Farm, HARTLAND, Near Bideford. Devon, EX39 6DU	0237 441238	234 246	April – October	11
Mrs Cornish, Leddon Farm, Darracott, WELCOMBE, Devon	0288 83380	231 178	All year	12

Name and Address	Telephone No.	Map Ref.	Site Open (Dates inclusive)	Section
NORTH CORNWALL				
Upper Lynstone Camping & Caravan Park, BUDE, EX23 0LP.	0288 352017	205 053	Easter – End September	12
2 Mrs S Weller, Hentervene C & C Park, CRACKINGTON HAVEN, Near Bude, EX23 0LF.	0840 230365	155 944	All year	13
Dennis Cove Campsite, PADSTOW, PL28 8DR.	0841 532349	920 745	Easter – End September	18
Carnevas Farm Holiday Park, PORTHCOTHAN BAY, Nr. St Merryn, PL28 8PN.	0841 520230	863 725	April – End October	20
4 Trevornick Holiday Park, HOLYWELL BAY, Newquay.	0637 830531		Easter – End September	21
Trevella Caravan & Camping Park, CRANTOCK, Newquay, TR8 5EW.	0637 830308		Open all year	22
Beacon Cottage Farm Touring Park, Beacon Drive, ST AGNES, TR5 0NU.	0872 552347	705 505	Easter – October	24
5 Manor Farm Caravan Site, Tehidy, PORTREATH, Camborne.	0209 713367	632 427	March – October	26
Mr C White, St Ives Bay Holiday Park, 73 Loggans Road, HAYLE, TR27 5BH.	0736 752274		Easter– End October	27
Mr M Osborne, Trevalgan Family Camping Park, ST IVES, TR26 3BJ.	0736 796433	490 402	May – End September	28
6. Kelynack Caravan & Camping Park, Kelynack, ST JUST, Penzance.	0736 787633	374 301	Easter – End October	29

0860   267385 .

0860 .   267398 .

Name and Address	Telephone No.	Map Ref.	Site Open (Dates inclusive)	Section
SOUTH CORNWALL				
X Treen Campsite, Treen, ST LEVAN, Penzance.	0736 810526	395 230	April – End October	33
Bone Valley Caravan Park, Heamoor, PENZANCE, TR20 8UJ.	0736 60313	462 318	March – mid December	34

SOUTH CORNWALL – continued

Name and Address	Telephone No.	Map Ref.	Site Open (Dates inclusive)	Section
Wheal Rodney, Gwallon, MARAZION, TR17 0HL.	0736 710605		April – October	35
Tenerife Farm Caravan & Camping Park, Attn. A B Thomas, Predannack, MULLION.	0326 240293	677 172	Easter – End September	38
Gwendreath Farm Caravan Park, KENNACK SANDS, Helston, TR12 7LZ.	0326 290666	729 167	Easter – October	40
Silver Sands Holiday Park, Gwendreath, KENNACK SANDS, Helston, TR12 7LZ.	0326 290631	729 169	Early April – End September	40
J B Jewell, Pennance Mill Farm, MAENPORTH, Falmouth, TR11 5HJ.	0326 312616	791 307	April – End October	42
Tremorvah Tent Park, SWANPOOL, Falmouth, TR11 5BE.	0326 312103	799 312	May – End September	42
Trewince Manor, Trewince, PORTSCATHO, Truro, TR2 5ET.	0872 58289	868 338	31 March – 31 October	44
Trelispen Camping Park, GORRAN HAVEN, St Austell.	0726 843501	005 421	Easter – End October	47
Sun Valley Holiday Park, Pentewan Road, ST AUSTELL, PL26 6DJ.	0726 843266		April – End October	50
Carlyon Bay Camping Park, Bethesda, Carlyon Bay, CHARLESTOWN, St Austell, PL25 3RE.	0726 812735	053 525		50
Kiligarth Manor Hols. Est., POLPERRO, PL13 2JQ	0503 72216	215 516	Easter – End September	52
Whitsand Bay Holiday Park, Millbrook, CAWSAND, Nr. Torpoint, PL10 1JZ.	0752 822597	410 514	Easter – October	55

SOUTH DEVON

Name and Address	Telephone No.	Map Ref.	Site Open (Dates inclusive)	Section
Higher Rew Farm Camping Park, MARLBOROUGH, Nr. Salcombe, TQ7 3DW.	0548 842681	714 383	Easter – October	60
Camping & Caravanning Club Site, Middle Grounds, SLAPTON, Torcross, TQ7 1QW.	0548 580538	825 450	April – September	61/62

7.

Name and Address	Telephone No.	Map Ref.	Site Open (Dates inclusive)	Section
SOUTH DEVON – continued				
Leonards Cove, STOKE FLEMING, Dartmouth, TQ6 0NR.	0803 770206	864 483	March – October	62
Beverly Park Holiday Park, Goodrington Road, PAIGNTON.	0803 843887	886 582	1 April — 31st October	64
Marine Park Holiday Centre, Grange Road, PAIGNTON.	0803 843887	886 587	1 June – 31st October	64
Cofton Farm Caravan & Camping Park, STARCROSS, Near Dawlish.	0626 890358		Easter – End October	66
Ladram Bay Caravan Site, LADRAM BAY, Nr Budleigh Salterton, Budleigh, EX9 7BX	0395 568398	096 854	April – End September	68
Oakdown Caravan Parks, WESTON, Nr Sidmouth, EX10 0PH.	02980 387	167 902	April – October	68
Manor Farm Camping & Caravan Site, Seaton Down Hill, SEATON, EX12 2JA.	0297 21524		1st April – 15th November	69
DORSET				
Manor Farm Holiday Centre, CHARMOUTH, Bridport, DT6 6QL.	0297 60226		All year	71
Newlands Camping Park, CHARMOUTH, DT6 6RB.	0297 60259	373 935	16 March – 31 October	71
Wood Farm Caravan, & Camping Park Axminster Road, CHARMOUTH, DT6 6BT.	0297 60697	355 940	April – October	71
Eype House Caravan & Camping Park, EYPE, Bridport, Dorset, DT6 6AL.	0308 24903	446 912	Easter Mid October	72
Freshwater Caravan Park, BURTON BRADSTOCK, Nr Bridport, DT6 4PT.	0308 897317	898 479	13 March – 13 November	73
Pebble Bank Caravan Park, c/o Camp Road, Wyke Regis, WEYMOUTH, DT4 9HF.	0305 774844	657 775	April – October	74
Durdle Door Caravan Park, Lulworth Cove, WEST LULWORTH, BH20 5PU	092941 200	811 808	April – October	75

SOUTH WEST WAY ASSOCIATION – HISTORY

We are sometimes asked what we have done and we set out below some of the things in which we have been involved in one way or another. We do as well send a steady flow of reports on path deficiencies, both as regards maintenance and the route of the path to the local authorities and the Countryside Commission.

1973   Official Formation in May.
Attendance Cornish Opening at Newquay.
Comments to Sports Council on proposed Countryside Park at Northam Burrows.
First Information Sheets produced.

1974   Evidence submitted to Mr Yapp for his report to the Countryside Commission on Long Distance Footpaths.
We welcomed Devon N.F.U. representation on our Committee.
Attendance at South Devon and Dorset Opening in September at Beer.
Registration as a Charity.
First Description issued.

1975   Mark Richard's book "Walking the North Cornwall Coastal Path" published – a work in which we may fairly say we played a part.
Small new section of Coast Path agreed at Clematon Hill, Bigbury at S.W.W.A.'s instigation.
Article on S.W.W. in Rucksack.
Attendance at Opening of so-called Exmoor Coastal Path.
Bideford Public Enquiry – successful opposition to Golf Course on the Coastal Path at Abbotsham.
Success at last in getting unstable path south from Hartland Point over Blagdon and Upright Cliffs.
Walk over new Lulworth Range Walk.

1976   First Footpath Guide issued.
Diversion at Thurlestone opposed.
Thanks to the Hon. Alan Clark M.P. an attempt to get Countryside Commission adjudged by Ombudsman; unfortunately, Countryside Commission outside his purview.
Evidence submitted to House of Commons Expenditure Committee Environment sub-committee.
Improvements at North Cliffs between Portreath and Hayle secured, thanks to National Trust.
Public Enquiry with R.A. at Kingswear on the section Kellys Cove to Mann Sands.
Consulted by Devon County Council on path at Watermouth and Dorset County Council about Abbotsbury.
Goodbye to our first Chairman, Mr Walter – we lose a tower of strength.

1977   S.W.W.A. mentioned in the Y.H. Handbook.
Publications of Letts Guides in three volumes. The first satisfactory books to whole path in which we can say our information helped a little.
Attendance at Coverack Youth Hostel official opening.
Evidence presented to Lord Porchester's Exmoor Study.
Badges produced.
Evidence given to Devon County Council for Taw/Torridge Estuary Survey.

1978   First Printed Footpath guide.
Attendance at Westward Ho! Somerset/North Devon Opening.
Opposition to diversion at Dean Quarry, St Keverne, Cornwall.
Lack of Path at Pentewan submitted to Local Ombudsman.
New path seaward of Radar Station at Hartland obtained, thanks to South West Way Association.

1979   Evidence given at Public Enquiries at Abbotsbury and Lulworth Cove.
Submission to Mr Himsworth for his report on Areas of Outstanding Natural Beauty.
First printed News Letters and Descriptions, and the first illustrated description.
Pine Haven to Port Quin gap submitted to Local Ombudsman.
Assistance to Letts for their Guide reprint.

1980   Result of 1976 Public Enquiry at Kingswear published.
Discussion Dean Quarry, St Keverne, Cornwall.
Dialogues with Countryside Commission about path deficiencies.
Alternative coastal path open Glenthorne Estate, Somerset and we submit proposals for rerouting in Exmoor National Park.
Special report submitted on St Loy, Cornwall.
Attendance at Widmouth Head, North Devon, Public Enquiry.
Opinions expressed to Department of Environment on draft "Wildlife and Countryside Bill".

1981   Annual Guide "State of the Path" section improved.
Attendance at second Kingswear Public Enquiry.
Countryside Commission decide that path wardenship will be greatly extended.
Bridge provided at Duckpool, North Cornwall.
Path improvements at Watermouth; Braunton to Barnstaple; Dean Quarry; Clematon Hill; Bigbury; Mothecombe and Maidencombe.

1982   Wardenship of coastal path in Cornwall completed.
Further openings at: Cleave Farm in North Cornwall, Pentewan with its unfortunate exe cution and Mount Edgecombe in South Cornwall, Higher Brownstone Farm, Kingswear and a short section west of Berry Head in South Devon.
Agreement was also reached for a high tide route at Mothecombe in South Devon.
The 1982 Guide incorporates a new 'Itinerary Suggested' section.

1983   Opening of the Widmouth Head section in North Devon and a second long section in South Devon between Kingswear and Mann Sands.
Major improvements to the Path on the western side of Crackington Haven, North Cornwall.
Cornwall's 10th Anniversary Walk.

1984   **New Section**
A new section of the Path opened on the east bank of the mouth of the River Dart close to Kingswear and giving access to Mill Bay Cove and a splendid stretch of coastal walking.

Improvement
A coastal route was opened westwards from Trebarwith Strand to Backways Cove in North Cornwall.

1985   **Improvement**
There was an improvement to the Dawlish/Teignmouth section of the path between Smugglers Lane and Windward Lane where the path has been removed from the main road.

Culbone – Foreland Point
The alternative coastal path at the Glenthorne Estate was waymarked as the official route, which is a great improvement.

Pinehaven – Port Quin (North Cornwall)
The new path was opened and is a vast improvement, although the substantial fence and barbed wire detracts from the scene.

1986   **Minehead to Porlock Weir** New alternative path between North Hill and Hurlstone Point signposted and waymarked.

Black Head, Cornwall Now purchased by the National Trust.

1987   **Barnstaple/Bideford/Northam** The new route completed along the railway lines and open.

Bude Attendance at Public Enquiry to prevent development adjacent to footpath.

Chynhalls Point Coastpath moved to seaward of hotel.

Branscombe Attendance at Public Enquiry to urge true coast path instead of inland route. Preferred route adopted.

Bidna/Northam Owing to breach in sea wall an acceptable diversion negotiated.

1988 **Woody Bay to Trentishoe** Devon County Council adopts our recommended, nearer the coast route as the official coast path.

1989 **Culbone** On site exploration with Countryside Commission and Exmoor National Park Authority to discover an acceptable alternative to the long unnecessary Culbone diversion.

Chynhalls Cliff On site exploration for a more coastal trail.

Fire Beacon Point/Pentargon Cornwall County Council install grand new path.

Wembury Attend public meeting at Down Thomas to successfully oppose erection of locked gates across Coast Path by Royal Navy.

Strete Gate/Warren Cove Attend public meeting and give evidence to support proposals by Countryside Commission and Devon County Council for an improved and more true coast path.

1990 **Membership** Now over 1000.

1991 **Buckator** At our request Cornwall County Council re-route offical path around the headland.

Worthy/Culbone On site explorations for a preferable diversion to that proposed by Exmoor National Park Authority.

Strete Gate/Warren Cove Continuing our strong argument with Devon County Council for a coast path.

Lyme Regis Continued pleas to Dorset County Council to reinstate the coast path along the golf course.

Total length we estimate the Coast Path to be about 613 miles long.

1992 Our recommended route between Watcombe and Maidencombe put in by Devon County Council.

Our suggested path at Worthygate Wood installed by National Trust.

Commenced discussions with Countryside Commission to examine sections of coast suitable for 'Set Aside'.

1993 Successful opposition to an application to close path on west side of Foreland Point.

Success with our request for a coast path avoiding the holiday complex at Buck's Mills.

Our suggested path installed by National Trust at Port Quin.

Write and produce the 'trail description' in this book the 'Other Way Round'.

INVITATION TO MEMBERSHIP

The South West Way is interesting in that it is not a modern idea like the Pennine Way; until 1913, it was an established working path patrolled on foot daily. The rows of coastguard cottages and old stone stiles remaining in many places are evidence of this usage. The Path when finished will run from Minehead in Somerset right round the South West Peninsula as far as Poole Harbour in Dorset. It will be the longest of the Long Distance Paths and more than twice the length of the Pennine Way – over 600 miles in fact.

The splendid idea of making this old path around the South West Peninsula one of the first of a series of Long Distance Paths came from a war-time committee of the Ramblers Association. The idea was put into effect by being included in the National Park and Access to the Countryside Act of 1949. In other words, Long Distance Footpaths have an equal basis in law with the much better known National Parks. Unfortunately, for the Long Distance Footpaths, they have largely been treated as poor relations ever since. The proof of this is, despite being authorised by Act of Parliament so long ago and despite several Opening Ceremonies, the South West Way is still unfinished.

The South West Way Association was formed after some months' preliminary work in May 1973. It is an independent body but works in co-operation with the Ramblers Association. The South West Way Association's first aim is to secure completion of the path.

Furthermore, the South West Way Association believe the Countryside Commission have been in error in two respects. Firstly, they have not made it a continuous path despite their own words: "There should be a continuous right of way along the entire length of the path." (Countryside Commission's National Long Distance Path – Some Questions Answered.)

Secondly, in several places, the Path has been diverted from the coast for no apparent good reason, even on occasions , on to main roads with no pavement. The South West Way Association believe it would be scenically more beautiful, less hindrance to agriculture and physically safer if kept on the coast. Experience has shown that diversions away from it are on the whole not satisfactory.

It seems that no local walking organizations were ever consulted about the path until South West Way Association came into being. Being reasonable people we cannot expect to have everything our own way – in fact there are many legitimate interests to consider. However, to establish a path without discussing it with the people who know it best, which is exactly what the Countryside Commission were apparently trying to do, seems altogether wrong.

The South West Way Association believe that, in a tourist-orientated area such as the South West, a continuous coastal path will be a major asset. It hopes the Path will bring more business to less frequented places and relieve some of the pressure on the South West National Parks. There are a great number of bodies interested in various parts of the Path. The South West Way Association believes it is important that it should represent all sections, and view the Path as a whole.

For further details of the type of work we do, see South West Way Association's History.

Members receive a free Annual Guide, two Newsletters a year with up-to-date information and a free copy of each new footpath description as it is issued.

A membership form is provided below.

NAME ....

(Block capital, please)

ADDRESS ....

....

Subscriptions: £7.00; Joint £8.00

Associations, Local Authorities £10.00; Life Subscription £100.00;

Joint £120.00

Please send to   Mrs M. Macleod, Membership Secretary,

                       South West Way Association,

                       1 Orchard Drive, Kingskerswell, Newton Abbot,

                       Devon TQ12 5DG. Telephone: (0803) 873061